John Steinbeck:

A Concise Bibliography (1930-65)

Compiled
by
Tetsumaro Hayashi
Kent State University

Introduction by Warren G. French

The Scarecrow Press, Inc.
Metuchen, N. J.   1967

To

Professor Hisashi Toda,

Professor Masato Yano,

Dr. Lalia P. Boone,

and

Dr. William L. Moore

Introduction

By Warren French

Bibliography is one of the least appreciated of gentle
callings. Zealous New Critics especially scoffingly dismiss
it as antiquarianism. How often in hatchet sessions behind
closed academic doors have I heard the volcanic personality
that erupts notes illuminating recondite symbols dismiss an
industrious, self-exacting colleague as "only a bibliographer."

But without the labors of the bibliographer any literary province remains a trackless wilderness--perhaps to be
eventually abandoned as a waste land, perhaps to be culti-
vated into fields whose rich deep soil will nourish centuries.
The bibliographer is the surveyor who imposes the order
that makes possible the systematic exploitation of a hitherto
unplumbed tract.

The first occupants of such a tract--to apply the meta-
phor particularly to the works of John Steinbeck, scholarly
scouts like Peter Lisca, Joseph Fontenrose and myself--
have sought only to appropriate for their own use what they
hoped would prove the richest fields or heights commanding
the most satisfying views, building their own houses and dig-
ging their own wells, without bothering much even to inspect
the abandoned campsites of pioneers like Harry T. Moore
and Edmund Wilson, who had chosen not to tarry.

A few inquirers interested in the area have beaten
paths to Professor Lisca's door and mine, but that tract labeled "Steinbeck Country" has remained largely a mysterious,
uncharted place, full of startling vistas, deeply secret places,
rocky outcroppings, nettles among wild roses. For a variety
of technical reasons, no early appraisals of the land have
carried complete reference maps. Even when the agreeabil-
ity of the annexation of this tract to Academia was signalled
by the publication of the reports of Maurice Beebe's advance
party in a special Steinbeck number of Modern Fiction Studies (Spring, 1965--a matter of only months ago), documenta-
tion was necessarily highly selective. The intrepid young
adventurer into Steinbeckland had still to rely almost exclu-

sively on his own resources--stout legs, sharp eyes, a good ear, a ready wit.

But as the landscape that the novelist created won gradually all the honors the unfancied world outside might bestow (Pulitzer Prize; Nobel Prize; Medal of Freedom), it became apparent that it could not much longer remain the preserve of its early settlers; as the demand for teachers of literature mounts, as graduate schools burgeon, as the "modern" literature of the twenties and thirties moves toward "classic" status, a mob of homesteaders gathers at the border waiting to rush this Oklahoma of the mind. But they need maps. Mr. Hayashi has provided for their needs.

This bibliography is truly a labor of love. Mr. Hayashi's own field is not modern American fiction; he explains his private enthusiasm for Steinbeck in his preface. No one expects to grow rich or famous on the strength of a bibliography. A visitor to our country, he has perceived a need that we have been too distractedly busy to fill ourselves, and he has provided us with a map that will vastly facilitate the subdivision of a wild tract of imagination into neat communities of the mind.

As the bibliographer acknowledges, his work is far from exhaustive. Many obscure and fugitive reprints of Steinbeck's work remain to be located; I have added after my last perusal of the bibliography, records of several interesting war-time paperback reprintings. Mr. Hayashi has also wisely chosen not to enter the enormous thickets-- bristling with problems--of foreign language editions and criticisms of Steinbeck. A vast amount of work remains to be done, and help is solicited. Someday we are led to believe that students in the humanities as well as the sciences will have at their disposal a vast information retrieval system that may render superfluous long, lonely labors like Mr. Hayashi's; but that day is not yet and our needs are urgent.

Urgent especially, because now more than a quarter of a century after what seems indisputably the height of Steinbeck's career, he remains the most controversial literary figure of his generation. Despite occasional mutterings, there is really no longer any disputing the status of Faulkner and Hemingway; and the battle for Scott Fitzgerald seems won, as that for James Farrell, for example, seems lost. Yet today in a college course in modern fiction, of two sensitive and perceptive students who generally agree on things

vi

literary, one can say that The Grapes of Wrath is superficial and monotonous, while the other finds that it provides a profound and moving experience.

Their difference of opinion reflects a division in the scholarly community between those who consider Steinbeck a mere journalist and those who adjudge him one of the masters of modern prose. Since the assessment of the world that Steinbeck has made is far from settled, it is especially important that we have tools that will acquaint newly recruited laborers with the scope and present status of the task.

This bibliography, although necessarily tentative, has at least one special value that even many definitive reference works lack. I especially welcome the inclusion of the detailed descriptions of manuscript holdings of Steinbeckana. One of the most bedlamite features of American scholarship is the fierce competition among prestige-seeking libraries for the contents of the wastebaskets of the great. Scholarship would be better served if these resources could be concentrated in some institution devoted to the principle of scholarly co-operation rather than fierce proprietorship; but if the spoils must remain divided, at least detailed analyses like Mr. Hayashi's assist the curious scholar who cannot roam freely to determine what and where they are.

The provision at last of this long awaited survey actually produces mixed feelings in those of us who have worked toward its compilation. Just as the early residents of a particularly attractive tract resent the coming of subdividers, so we feel a certain regret at seeing a literary province we once regarded as a private preserve become cluttered with homesteaders; but these regrets are short-lived, for the pioneering mind is never really content to rest--attractive new lands are opening up, and we must move on--ahead of the rest--to the territories being created by James Purdy or John Barth, pausing only to shout to the newcomers, "Welcome to Steinbeckland," and pressing upon them Mr. Hayashi's guide to its mysteries, pitfalls, and wonders.

Kansas City, Missouri

April, 1966

Preface

My personal interest in John Steinbeck began in 1957 when I was first introduced to The Grapes of Wrath by Dr. Harry R. Warfel, the distinguished scholar of American literature. I had the privilege then of taking his Seminar on American Prose at the University of Florida. I began reading other works of Steinbeck on my own after this initial encounter and eventually began to write some articles about this great American author.

When I read Steinbeck's Travels With Charley In Search of America in 1962, I felt as if I were meeting the author in person. Within a year he was honored with the Nobel Prize for literature. At that time the author himself expressed a sense of surprise at the honor, but enthusiastic readers at home and abroad knew that it had been long overdue. He seems to me one of the American authors who has been underestimated and misjudged by his own countrymen. He is still one of the controversial literary figures. However, his talents as a spokesman of American culture and conscience, as a great artist, and as a profound thinker are gaining increased recognition.

As far as I know, there has not been a comprehensive bibliography published to date. It is certainly true that an author of Steinbeck's stature deserves an established scholar to compile such a bibliography. It is my sincere hope, therefore, that this work may lead to more extensive critical bibliographies for advanced studies.

John Steinbeck seems, to some critics at least, to have already reached his peak as a writer, perhaps with the award of the Nobel Prize, but the true evaluation and critical appraisal of his art has just begun. I do not claim for a moment that this bio-bibliography is perfect. I shall welcome and appreciate any additions and corrections which the users of this book may suggest.

Some of the sources presented here were discovered personally. For many others I have made use of standard

ix

bibliographical aids as well as the selected bibliographies prepared by various scholars of American literature. I owe the editors and compilers of these reference books special thanks.

I could never have finished this book without the assistance, criticism, and encouragement of many scholars, librarians, and friends. I wish to express my appreciation especially to Dr. Warren G. French, a leading Steinbeck scholar, who was most enthusiastic in endorsing my project by giving me valuable suggestions, and by writing the introduction to this book; to Mr. Preston Beyer, an outstanding Steinbeck collector who informed me of many editions of Steinbeck's works as well as of critical materials; to Dr. Irene Zimmerman, Dr. Lalia P. Boone, and Dr. Lotte Graeffe, of the University of Florida, who first endorsed my project and gave me specific advice and moral support; and to Professor Sakae Morioka, editor of Kyushu American Literature, who was kind enough to select for me representative Steinbeck articles published in the English language in Japan. I would like also to recognize Dr. James Salem who has assisted me with the organization of this book and made many valuable suggestions concerning the publication of this bibliography. From the faculty and staff of Kent State University I wish to recognize Professor Edward G. McGehee, Mr. Dean Keller, Miss Dorothy Green, Professor John B. Nicholson, Jr., Miss Julia Waida, and Miss Virginia Crowl who gave me constructive criticism and helpful suggestions. My thanks go also to the following institutions for providing me with Steinbeck materials or the information of them: The Connecticut State Prison Library (Mr. Steinbeck was not in prison!), the Connecticut State Library, the Monterey Public Library, Stetson University Library, and Cleveland Public Library. In addition I am indebted to the following publishers for giving me various examination copies of Steinbeck materials: Bantam Books, Cliff's Notes, Dell Publishing Company, Humanities Research Center of the University of Texas, Monarch Press, Scott, Foresman & Co., and Viking Press.

In compiling a list of Steinbeck manuscripts I am much obliged and most grateful to Dr. Warren G. French, Miss Dorothy Green, Professor John B. Nicholson, Jr., the compilers of American Literary Manuscripts, and the librarians of the twenty-one institutions, for their assistance, suggestions, and criticism.

In general I followed Kate L. Turabian's bibliographical method; however, I took the liberty of adding or revising some of the entries whenever I thought it beneficial to the users of this bibliography.

Tetsumaro Hayashi
Kent State University
January, 1966

Table of Contents

Chronology

1902

John Ernst Steinbeck born February 27 in Salinas, California.

1919

Graduated from Salinas High School.

1920

Began intermittent attendance at Stanford University.

1924

First publication, "Fingers of Cloud" and "Adventures in Arcademy," in The Stanford Spectator (February and June).

1925

Left Stanford permanently without a degree.
Went to New York City and worked as construction laborer and reporter of The American (newspaper).

1926

Returned to California.
Humorous verses published in Stanford Lit:
1. "If Eddie Guest Had Written the Book of Job: Happy Birthday,"
2. "If John A. Weaver Had Written Keats' Sonnet in the American Language: On Looking at a New Book by Harold Bell Wright,"
3. "Atropos: Study of a Very Feminine Obituary Editor."

1929

Cup of Gold published.

1930

Married Carol Henning and began residence in Pacific Grove.
First met Edward F. Ricketts.

1932

Moved to Los Angeles in summer.
The Pastures of Heaven published.

1933

Returned to Pacific Grove early in year.

To a God Unknown published.
Two stories, the first two parts of The Red Pony
("The Gift" and "The Great Mountains") published in
North American Review in November and December.
(Later included in LV.)

1934

Oliver Hamilton Steinbeck, John's mother died in
February.
"The Murder" selected as an O. Henry prize story
and published in O. Henry Prize Stories.
"The Raid" published in North American Review
(Both in LV.)

1935

Tortilla Flat published, bringing immediate fame and
financial success.
Won the Commonwealth Club of California Gold Medal.
Cited as "the Year's Best By a Californian."
Verses, "Mammy," "Baubles," "To a Carmel,"
"The Visitor," "Four Shades of Navy Blue," "The
Genius," "Ivanhoe," "Thoughts on Seeing a Stevedore"
published in Monterey Beacon.
"The White Qual" published in North American Review.
(Later in LV.)
"The Snake" published in Monterey Beacon. (LV)

1936

In Dubious Battle published.
The California Novel of 1936 Prize for the novel.
Moved to Los Gatos, California.
His father, John Ernst Steinbeck, died in May.
Articles, "The Harvest Gypsies," published in San
Francisco News in October.
Trip to Mexico.

1937

Of Mice and Men published in February.
Went to New York and Pennsylvania to work on stage
version, which was produced at Music Box Theatre
in New York in November and won Drama Critics'
Circle Silver Plaque for that season.
Chosen one of the ten outstanding young man of the
year.
The Red Pony, in three parts, published.
First trip to Europe.
Later in year, went to West from Oklahoma with mi-

grants.
"The Promise" and "The Ears of Johnny Bear" published in Harper's Magazine. (Later in LV.)

1938

The Long Valley and Their Blood is Strong, pamphlet reprint of "The Harvest Gypsies" (Article) published.
"The Harness" published in The Atlantic Monthly. (LV.)

1939

The Grapes of Wrath published.
National Institute of Arts and Letters membership given.

1940

The Grapes of Wrath won (1) Pulitzer Prize, (2) American Book-sellers Association Award, and (3) Social Work Today Award.
With Edward F. Ricketts went to Gulf of California on "Western Flyer" to collect marine invertebrates, March-April.
Filmed The Forgotten Village in Mexico. (The book published in 1941.)

The Grapes of Wrath (1939) filmed.
Of Mice and Men (1937) filmed.

1941

The Forgotten Village published.
"How Edith McGillicuddy Met Robert Louis Stevenson" published in Harper's Magazine. (Later in Portable Steinbeck.)

1942

Separation and interlocutory divorce from Carol Henning.
The Moon is Down (novel and play) published.
Bombs Away written for Army Air Corps.
Tortilla Flat filmed.

1943

Married Gwyn Conger in March and began residence in New York.
Spent several months in European war zone as correspondent for New York Herald Tribune.
The Moon is Down filmed.

1944

    Son Thomas born.
    In December Lifeboat filmed.

1945

    Cannery Row published.
    The Red Pony republished with fourth chapter, "The
    Leader of the People."
    "The Pearl of the World" appeared in Woman's Home
    Companion magazine in December.
    A Medal for Benny filmed.
    Bought home in New York.

1946

    Won King Haakon (Norway) Liberty Cross for The
    Moon is Down.
    A filmscript, "A Medal for Benny" published.
    Son John born.

1947

    Trip to Russia with Robert Capa, August-September.
    The Wayward Bus published.
    The Pearl published and filmed.
    Norwegian Award for The Moon is Down.
    The Wayward Bus selected as The Book-of-the-
    Month Club book.

1948

    Elected to American Academy of Letters.
    Divorced from Gwyn Conger.
    A Russian Journal with Robert Capa, an account of
    his trip to Russia, published.
    Edward F. Ricketts died.
    A short story, "Miracle of Tepayac" published in
    Collier's.

1949

    The Red Pony filmed.
    A short story, "His Father" published in Reader's Di-
    gest.

1950

    Burning Bright (novel and play) published.
    Married to Elaine Scott in December.
    Viva Zapata! filmed.

1951

    The Log From the Sea of Cortez published, containing introduction and narrative from Sea of Cortez and biography of Edward F. Ricketts.

1952

East of Eden published.
Sent reports to Collier's from Europe.

1954

Sweet Thursday published.

1955

Pipe Dream (Richard Rodgers and Oscar Hammerstein II musical comedy based on Sweet Thursday) produced.
Editorials for Saturday Review.
East of Eden (1952) filmed.

1956

The O. Henry Award for "Affair at 7, Rue de M. ....."

1957

The Short Reign of Pippin IV published.
The Wayward Bus (1947) filmed.

1958

Once There Was a War, a collection of wartime dispatches, published.

1961

The Winter of Our Discontent published.
The Book-of-the-Month Club selected The Winter of Our Discontent.
"Flight" (a short story) filmed in San Francisco and independently produced.

1962

Travels With Charley published.
Received Nobel Prize for Literature in December.

1964

John F. Kennedy Memorial Library Trusteeship given.
Won Press Medal of Freedom and United States Medal of Freedom.

Part I   Primary Material

A. Novels
Burning Bright.
New York: Viking Press, 1950.

Bantam: H 2936
New Bantam: F 2396, 1962.

Cannery Row.
New York: Viking Press, 1945.

American Services Edition: T 5
Bantam: FC 196, 1947
Viking (Compass C 131), 1945.
See I, E.

The Cup of Gold: A Life of Henry Morgan, Buccaneer,
with occasional references to history.
New York: Robert M. McBride, 1929.

Armed Services Editions: 750 (Preface by Lewis Gan-
nett.)
Bantam: H 2805
Covici-Friede, 1936, new edition, Maroon cloth d.w.,;
another Covici-Friede edition, 1936, Blue cloth, d.w.
Popular Library Edition: 216

East of Eden.
New York: Viking Press, 1952.

Viking Limited Edition.   Autographed by the author.
Limited to 1,500 copies of which 750 are for private
distribution.

A movie of the same title was filmed by Warner Bros.
in 1955.

Bantam: 1954, 1955: F 1267; N 2937, 1962
Grosset
Reader's Digest Association: Chapter 34 from East of

Eden was privately printed on hand press of Valenti
Angelo at Bronxville, N. Y.   125 copies.
Reader's Digest Condensed Books 1953 selections
Sears Reader's Club (Chicago), 1953.

The Grapes of Wrath.
New York: Viking Press, 1939.

Movie of the same title by 20th Century-Fox Film
Corp. , 1940.

American R. D. M. Corp. (New York), 1963.
Armed Services Edition: 290
Bantam: N 2710, 1945
Diners' Club International Collectors' Library, 1965
A gold-stamped replica binding, pseudo-deluxe edi-
tion for Diners' Club's members only.
Heritage Press Edition with lithographs by Thomas
Hart Benton, with preface by Joseph Henry Jackson,
New York, 1940.
Limited Editions Club   2 vols. , 1940
Lithograph; the advance announcement of the
The Grapes of Wrath, The Wind in the Willows,
and The Decameron.
Living Library Edition.   World Pub. Co. , 1947
Introduced by Carl Van Doren.
Modern Library, 1941
Thor Publications, 1964
Viking (Compass C33), 1958.

In Dubious Battle.
New York: Covici-Friede, 1936
99 deluxe copies, numbered and signed by the author.

Bantam: H 2279, S 2952, 1961
Modern Library: 115, 1939
Sun Dial Press, 1940
Viking (Compass C 132), 1963.

The Moon is Down.
New York: Viking Press, 1942.
700 copies bound in paper for distribution exclusively
to booksellers.

Bantam: F 2711; Fighting Forces Penguine Special Edition
(S-219), 1943.
Sun Dial Press, 1943
Also with Charles Dickens' Tales of Two Cities, ed.
by Edgar M. Schuster. New York: Noble, 1961.

Of Mice and Men.
New York: Covici-Friede, 1937.
2,500 copies were printed. Page 9, lines 2-3 from the bottom of the page reads "and only moved because the heavy hands were/pendula." This was removed in later printings. Text of the Book-of-the-Month Club copies is identical to the second printing.

Bantam: FC 240, 1955
Modern Library, 1938; Triangle Books, 1938.
Viking (Compass C 125), 1963.

The Pastures of Heaven.
New York: Brewer, Warren and Putnam, 1932.

Armed Services Edition: 703
Avon Modern Age Books: 20, 1945
    Contains "Nothing So Monstrous" and "The Hanging at San Quentin."
Avon: 25 10 Great Short Stories, 1945
Avon Modern Short Story Monthly: 31, 1946
    Contains "Molly Morgan."
Bantam: H 2940, 1951
Modern Age Books; Penguine Books, 1942.
Seal Book: 43, 1938
Viking (Compass C 133), 1963
World Publishing Co., Tower Book T 254, 1946.

The Pearl.
New York: Viking Press, 1947.

Movie by RKO Radio Pictures, Inc., 1947.

Bantam: EP 78, 1962
With George Eliot's Silas Maner, Ed. by W. Greene.
    New York: Noble, 19??
In Exploring Life Through Literature, Ed. by Robert L. Pooley, et al. (Gr. 10), Scott, 1964. pp. 631-673.
In Omnibook, 1948.

The Short Reign of Pippin IV: A Fabrication.
New York: Viking Press, 1957.

Bantam: F 2605, 1958

Sweet Thursday.
New York: Viking Press, 1954.

Bantam: FC 199, SC 273, 1961; FC 103, 1963; SC
273, 1965.

To a God Unknown.
New York: Robert O. Ballon, 1933.

Bantam: H 2804, 1955; A 1324, 1956
Covici-Friede, 1933; Dell Books, 1940(?)

Tortilla Flat.
Illustrated by Ruth Gannett.
New York: Covici-Friede, 1935.
500 copies were printed as prepublication copies.
Later editions so indicated on copyright page.
Filmed by Loew's Inc., 1942.

Bantam: H 3019, 1965
Modern Library: 216, 1937
New American Library; Signet P 2189
Pengin Books, 1946
Viking, 1947 (Illustrated by Peggy Worthington.)
Viking (Compass C 134), 1963.

The Wayward Bus.
New York: Viking Press, 1947.

Filmed by 20th Century-Fox, 1957.

Bantam: H 2894

The Winter of our Discontent.
New York: Viking Press, 1961.

Bantam: S 2461
Book-of-the-Month Club, 1961.

B. Plays and Filmscripts
Burning Bright (Acting Edition).
New York: Dramatists Play Service, 1951.

The Forgotten Village.
New York: Viking Press, 1941.

A story of conflict between modern medicine and

primitive supersitition in a Mexican village; a script
for a documentary filmed in Mexico.   See I, F (Non-
Fiction).

The Moon is Down: A Play in Two Parts.
New York: Viking Press, 1943.

Filmed by 20th Century-Fox Film Corp., 1943.
Abridged in The Best Plays of 1941-1942, ed. by
Robert B. Mantle.

New York: Dodd, Mead and Co., 1942, pp. 72-108.
Dramatists Play Service Edition

Of Mice and Men: A Play in Two Parts.
New York: Covici-Friede, 1937.
Filmed by Hal Roach Studio, Inc. (United Artists),
1940.
Abridged in The Best Plays of 1937-1938, Ed. by
Robert B. Mantle. New York: Dodd, Mead and Co.,
1938.   pp. 31-36.
Also in Famous American Plays of the 1930, Ed. by
Harold Churman.

Bantam: AC 12, 1958
Dell: 2478 LE
Also in Twenty Best Plays of the Modern American
Theatre, Ed. by John Gassner. New York: Crown
Publishers, 1941.   pp. 643-680.

C. Movies Based on Steinbeck's Works
East of Eden (1952)
Warner Bros., 1955.

"Flight", an unreleased motion picture version.
San Francisco, 1961.   Independently produced.

The Grapes of Wrath (1939)
20th Century-Fox Film Corp., 1940.

Lifeboat, Filmed by 20th Century-Fox Film Corp., 1944.
Steinbeck's script for Alfred Hitchcock's film, Lifeboat, which has never been published.

A Medal for Benny
Paramount, 1945.
A film script, 1946.

See II, B.

The Moon is Down (1942)
20th Century-Fox Film Corp., 1943.

Of Mice and Men (1937)
Hal Roach Studio, Inc., 1940.

The Pearl (1947)
RKO Radio Pictures, Inc., 1948.
Spanish (original) and English versions of the same
picture with the same cast and director.
The Spanish version is about 10 minutes longer.

Director: Emilio Fernandez
Cast: Pedro Armendariz; Mario Elena Marques;
Fernando Wagner; Charles Rooner.

The Red Pony (1937)
Chas. K. Feldman Group Productions and Lewis
Milestone Productions, 1949.

Tortilla Flat (1935)
Loew's Inc., 1942.

Viva Zapata!
Twentieth Century-Fox Film Corp., 1950.

Steinbeck's script for Marlon Brando's portrayal of
a Mexican revolutionary hero, Viva Zapata!

The Wayward Bus (1947)
20th Century-Fox Film Corp., 1957.

Cf.   Reader's Guide to Periodical Literature, (Movie
reviews)
International Motion Picture Almanac, and

Catalog of Copyright Entries: Motion Pictures
(Library of Congress)
for further information.

D. Adaptations of Steinbeck's Works
East of Eden:

Osborn, Paul (ed.), "Dialogue Script: East of Eden
Study of Current English (Tokyo), X (September 1955),

16-32.
(Screen play of Steinbeck's novel in English with
Japanese translation, continued from August issue.)

The Grapes of Wrath:

A screen play by Nunnally Johnson, based on the novel,
in Twenty Best Film Plays 1941-42, Ed. by John Gassner and Dudley Nichols. New York: Crown, 1943.
pp. 333-377.

The Leader of the People. Chicago: Dramatic, 1952.
   A dramatization by Luella E. McMahon of Steinbeck's
   short story.

A Medal for Benny, a screen play by Frank Butler,
   based on John Steinbeck and Jack Wagner's short
   story, in Best Film Plays, 1945, Ed. by John Gassner and Dudley Nichols. New York: Crown, 1946.
   pp 586-648.

Molly Morgan, based on story from The Pastures of
   Heaven, dramatized by Reginald Lawrence. New York:
   Dramatic, 1961. (Chicago: Dramatic, 1951)
   See II, A.

Pipe Dream (Musical comedy by Richard Rogers and
   Oscar Hammerstein II; the script of the Broadway
   musical play by Oscar Hammerstein II. Based on
   Sweet Thursday.) New York: Viking Press, 1954.

Viva Zapata. Screen play abridged in Argosy, XXXIII
   (February, 1952). Based on the Steinbeck-Elia Kazan
   movie. The pictures were taken on location along the
   Mexican border.

E. Short Stories
   "Adventures in Arcademy: A Journal into the Ridiculous,"
   The Stanford Spectator, II (June, 1924), 279, 291.

   "Affair at 7, Rue de M. ....," in Prize Stories
   1956: The O. Henry Awards, Ed. by Paul Engle and
   Hansford Martin. Garden City, N. Y.: Doubleday,
   1956. Reprinted from Harper's Bazaar.

"Breakfast, " Progressive Weekly, (n. v.) (May 6, 1939),
n. p.
Also in LV and Portable Steinbeck as well as in
Pacific Weekly, XV (November 9, 1936), n. p.
Also in Turning Point: Fourteen Great Tales of Dar-
ing and Decision, Ed. by George Bennett. New York:
Dell Pub. Co. , 1965. pp. 174-177.

"The Chrysanthemums, " Harper's, CLXXV (October,
1937), 513-519
Also in LV, Portable Steinbeck, and The Best Short
Stories of 1938, Ed. by Edward J. O'Brien. Boston:
Houghton Mifflin, 1938.

"Cutting Loose, " in collaboration with Michael Ratcliffe.
Encore, Ed. by Leonard Russell. London: Michael
Joseph Ltd. , 1963.

"Danny and His Friends, " in Portable Steinbeck and
A Treasury of Friendship, Comp. and Ed. by Ralph
L. Woods, New York: David McKay Co. , 1957.

"Death of Grampa, " in Taken at the Flood: The Human
Drama as Seen by Modern American Novelists, Ed.
by Ann Watkins. New York: Harper, 1946.

"Death Shall Be Paid, " in Portable Steinbeck.

"Dust" in Reading I've Liked, Ed. by C. Fadiman.
New York: Simon and Schuster, 1945.
See The Red Pony in II, A.

"The Ears of Johnny Bear, " Esquire, VIII (September,
1937), 35, 195-200.
Also in LV as "Johnny Bear";
Also in The Bedside Esquire, Ed. by A. Gingrich.
New York: Tudor Pub. Co. , 1937.

"Elf in Algiers, " in Pause to Wonder, Ed. by Marjorie
Fischer and Rolfe Humphries. Garden City, N. Y. :
Sun Dial Press, 1947; also by New York: Julian
Messner, Inc. , 1944. p. 401

"Fingers of Cloud: a Satire on College Proternity, "
Standard Spectator, II (February, 1924), 149, 161-164.

Also in Stanford Writers, 1891-1941, Ed. by Violet
L. Shue. Dramatists Alliance, Stanford University.
Limited to 30 copies.

"Flight," in LV and Portable Steinbeck.
Also in Adventures in American Literature, Ed. by
R. B. Inglis, et al. New York: Harcourt, Brace
and Co., 1951.
In Introduction to the Short Story: Study Materials,
Ed. by W. Boynton and Maynard Mack.
New York: Hayden Book Co., 1965.
Also in Short Story Masterpieces, Ed. by Robert
Penn Warren and Albert Erskine. New York: Dell
Pub. Co., 1954.

"The Gift," in Portable Steinbeck and The Red Pony.
Also in The Pocket Reader. New York: Pocket Books,
1941. p. 141.
See II, A.

"The Great Mountains," North American Review,
CCXXXVI (December, 1933), 492-500.
Also in LV and Portable Steinbeck.
In Two and Twenty, A Collection of Short Stories,
Ed. by R. H. Singleton. New York: St. Martin's,
1962. pp. 236-238; 236-238 contain some bio-
bibliographical information about Steinbeck.

Also in Accents, Ed. by Robert C. Pooley, et al (eds.)
Chicago: Scott, Foresman & Co., 1965. pp. 584-591.
See II, 3.

"The Hanging at San Quentin," in Avon, No. 20. 1945
(Modern Age Books, Short Story Monthly.)

"The Harness," Atlantic, CLXI (June, 1938), 741-749.
Also in LV and Portable Steinbeck.

"His Father," Reader's Digest, LV (September, 1949),
19-21.

"How Edith McGillcuddy Met Robert Louis Stevenson, "
Harper's, CLXXXIII (August, 1941), 252-258.
Also in Portable Steinbeck.
In Scholastic, XLIV (April 24, 1944), 21-22.
In Cleveland: Rowfant Club, 1943. Limited to 152
copies by Grabhorn Press, San Francisco, 1943.
Also in The Best American Short Stories of 1942,
Ed. by Martha Foley, Boston: Houghton Mifflin, 1952.
In The Best Short Stories of 1942, O. Henry Me-
morial Stories, Ed. by H. Brickell. New York:
Literary Guild, 1942.

"How Mr. Hogan Robbed a Bank, " Atlantic, CXCVII
(March, 1956), 58-61.
Also in Working With Prose, Ed. by Otto Reinert.
New York: Harcourt, Brace and Co., 1959. pp. 20-
30

"Johnny Bear, " in LV. (See "The Ears of Johnny Bear. ")
Also in Great Tales of the Far West. New York:
Lion Library, 1956. No. 88.

"The King Snake and the Rattles, " Brief, LXVI (April,
1953), 22-27.

"The Leader of the People, " in LV and Portable Stein-
beck.
Also in The Golden Argosy. New York: The Dial
Press, 1955.
Also in The Pocket Book of Modern American Short
Stories, Ed. by Philip Van Doren Stern. New York:
Pocket Books, Inc., 1943.
Also in This is My Best Edition, Ed. by Whit Burnett.
New York: Dial Press, 1942.
Also in The United States in Literature, Ed. by Wal-
ter Blair, et al (eds.). Chicago: Scott, Foresman &
Co., 1963. pp. 417-486.

"Lilli Marlene, " in The Best of the Diners' Club Magazine. New York: Regent American Pub. Co., 1962.
p. 322.

"The Lonesome Vigilante, " Esquire, VI (October, 1936),
35; 186A-186B.
Also in LV as "Vigilante, ";
The Bedside Esquire, Ed. by A. Gingrich. New York:
Tudor Pub. Co., 1937.

See "Vigilante. "

The Long Valley, including The Red Pony.
New York: Viking Press, 1938.

Armed Services Edition: 794; Avon Books, 1945.
Viking (Compass C1), 1956.
See I. J.

"Miracle of Tepayac, " Collier's, CXXII (December 25,
1948), 22-23.

"Molly Morgan, " in Portable Steinbeck.
Also in Avon, No. 31, 1946.

"Murder, " North American Review, CCXXXVII (April,
1934), 305-312.
Also in LV and O. Henry Prize Stories of 1934.
New York: Doubleday, Doran and Co. , 1934.
Also in The Bedside Tales, Introduced by Peter
Arno.   New York: William Penn Pub. , 1945.

"Nothing for Himself, " in Continent's End; A Collection
of California Writing, Ed. by Joseph Henry Jackson,
et al.   New York: McGraw-Hill, 1944.

"Nothing So Monstrous, " New York: Pynson Printers,
1936.
A reprint of the Junius Maltby story from The
Pastures of Heaven with illustration by Donald McKay
and an epilogue by the author written for this edition
of 370 un-numbered copies.
Also in Modern Age Books.   Avon, No. 20.
Short Story Monthly, 1945.

"Over the Hill, " in Half-a-Hundred; Tales by Great
American Writers, Ed. by C. Grayson. Toronto:
Blakiston, 1945.

11

"The Pearl of the World," Woman's Home Companion,
LXXII (December, 1945), 177ff.
See Part I-A. The Pearl.

"The Promise," Harper's, CLXXV (August, 1937), 243-
252.
Also in LV and Portable Steinbeck.
Part III of The Red Pony; O. Henry Prize Stories of
1938. New York: Doubleday, Doran and Co., 1938.

"The Raid," North American Review, CCXXXVIII
(October, 1934), 299-305.
Also in LV.

The Red Pony. New York: Covici-Friedi, 1937.
Set in monotype Italian Oldstyle and printed on hand-
made La Garde paper; 699 numbered copies were
printed by the Pynson Printers of New York under the
supervision of Elmer Adler, each copy signed by the
author, September, 1937.
I. The Gift
II. The Great Mountains
III. The Promise (The 1945 ed. includes IV. The
Leader of the People.)
See I, J.

Bantam: EP 79, 1948
Viking, 1959. Also included in LV. New York:
Viking Press, 1938.
Also in American Harvest: Twenty Years of Creative
Writing in the United States, Ed. by Allan Tale and
J. P. Bishop. Garden City, N. Y.: Doubleday, 1943.
Also in Anthology of Famous American Stories. New
York: Modern Library, 1953.
Also in Great Modern Short Stories. New York:
Modern Library, 1944.
Also in The Pocket Reader. New York: Pocket Books,
Inc., 1941. Labeled as The Red Pony, but includes
only "The Gift."
Also in Reading I've Liked, Ed. by C. Fadiman.

New York: Simon and Schuster, 1945.

Filmed by Charles K. Feldman Groups Production-
Lewis Milestone Productions, 1949.

"The Red Pony, " North American Review, **CCXXXVI**
(November, 1933), 421-438.
Also in LV as "The Gift" and Portable Steinbeck.

Saint Katy the Virgin. New York: Covici Friede, 1936.
199 numbered copies, signed by the author.
Also in LV.

"The Short-Short Story of Mankind, " in The Permanent
Play Boy, Ed. by Roy Russell. New York: Crown
Publishers, 1959. p. 325.

"The Snake, " Monterey Beacon, I (June 22, 1935),
10-14.
Also in LV.
Also in Great American Short Stories, Ed. by Wallace
and Mary Stagner. New York: Dell Pub. Co., 1957.

"A Snake of One's Own, " in The Bedside Esquire, Ed.
by Arnold Gingrich. New York: Tudor Pub. Co.,
1954.
Also in The Best, a Quarterly magazine, "a continu-
ing anthology of the world's greatest writing, "
New York: Macfadden-Bartell Corp. (Winter, 1965).

"Sons of Cyrus Trask, " Collier's, **CXXX** (July 12,
1952), 14-15.

"The Time the Wolves Ate the Vice Principal, " in
'47 The Magazine of the Year, I (March, 1947), 26-
27.
(An interchapter omitted from Cannery Row.)
See I, A.

"Tractored Off, " in Literature for Our Time; An
Anthology for College Freshmen, Ed. by Leonard
Stanley Brown, et al. New York: H. Holt and Co.,
1947.
Also in America in Literature, Ed. by Tremaine Mc-
Dowell. Madison, Wis.: F. S. Crofts and Co., for

the U. S. Armed Forces Institute, 1944.

"The Tractors, " in Our Lives; American Labor Stories,
Ed. by Joseph Gaer. New York: Boni and Gaer,
1948.

"The Turtle, " in Portable Steinbeck.
Also in Reading I've Liked, Ed. by C. Fadiman.
New York: Simon and Schuster, 1945.

"Vigilante, " in LV.
See "The Lonesome Vigilante. "

"The White Quail, " North American Review, CCXXXIX
(March, 1935), 204-211.
Also in LV.
Also in American Short Stories. Chicago: Scott,
Foresman and Co. , 1952.

F. Non-Fiction Miscellanies
America and Americans. New York: Viking, 1966.

Bombs Away: The Story of a Bomber Team.
Written for the U. S. Army Air Forces with 60
photographs by John Swope. New York: Viking Press,
1942.

Del Monte Recipes. Del Monte, California, 1937.
Issued by the Del Monte Properties Co. as a
promotion piece for the Hotel Del Monte. Steinbeck's favorite recipe is included among those of
other people. (Steinbeck's article) included

Famous Recipes by Famous People, Ed. by Herbert
Cermin. Illustrated by Sinclair Ross.
Published by Sunset Magazine in cooperation with
Hotel Del Monte, San Francisco, California.
"Of Beef and Men, " p. 11.

The Forgotten Village. New York: Viking Press, 1941.
A script for a documentary filmed in Mexico, with
136 photographs from the film of the same name by

Rosa Harvan Kleine and Alexander Hackensmid.
See I, B.

The Log From the Sea of Cortez. New York: Viking
Press, 1951.
The narrative portion of Sea of Cortez: A Leisurely
Journal of Travel and Research, 1941, with a profile
"About Ed Ricketts."

Viking (Compass C 120), 1951.
See Sea of Cortez.

Once There Was a War. New York: Viking Press,
1958.
A collection of Steinbeck's wartime dispatch to the
New York Herald Tribune.

Bantam: F 2979.

A Russian Journal, with Robert Capa as photographer.
New York: Viking Press, 1948.

Sea of Cortez: A Leisurely Journal of Travel and
Research, with Edward F. Ricketts.
New York: Viking Press, 1941.
See The Log From the Sea of Cortez.

Their Blood is Strong. San Francisco: Simon J.
Lubian Society of California, 1938.
(Pamphlet of articles published in San Francisco News,
October 5-12, 1936 as "The Harvest Gypsies.")

Travels With Charley in Search of America. New
York: Viking Press, 1962.

Bantam: S 258, 1963
Large Type Book Society Edition, 1966. (In prepa-
ration.)

G. Articles and Essays
"About Ed Ricketts," Preface to The Log From the
Sea of Cortez. New York: Viking Press, 1951.
pp. vii-lxvii.

"Aerial Engineer," Scholastic, XLIII (December 6, 1943),
17-18.

"Always Something to Do in Salinas," Holiday, XVII (June, 1955), 58ff.

An article by Steinbeck in Pascal Covici 1888-1964, Series of articles in tribute to Pascal Covici. Privately printed. Limited to 500 copies. Not for sale. p. 19.

"Atque Vale," Saturday Review, XLIII (July 23, 1960), 13.

"Black Man's Ironic Burden; Reprint," Negro History Bulletin, XXIV (April, 1961), 146ff.

"Bomber, Our Best Weapon," Science Digest, XIV (July, 1943), 61-63.

"Conversation at Sag Harbor," Holiday, XXIX (March, 1961), 60-61.

"Critics, Critics Burning Bright," Saturday Review, XXXIII (November 11, 1950), 20-21. Also as "My Short Novels," in SHC. pp. 38-42. Also in Bantam Book, 913, 1951. pp. 106-111. (A statement of Steinbeck's intention in Burning Bright and in other writings.)

"Critics from a Writer's Point of View," Saturday Review, XXXVIII (August 27, 1955), 20. Also in SHC as "Critics....from a Writer's Viewpoint." pp. 48-51.

"D for Dangerous," McCalls, LXXXV (October, 1957), 57ff.

"The Death of a Racket," Saturday Review, XXXVIII (April 2, 1955), 26.

"Dedication," The Journal of American Medical Association, CLXVII (July 12, 1958), 1388-1389. See "Spivacks Beat the Odds; condensed in The Reader's Digest.

"Dichos: the Way of Wisdom," Saturday Review, XL (November 9, 1957), 13.

"Discovering the People of Paris," Holiday, XX

(August, 1956), 36.

"Dubious Battle in California, " Nation, CXLIII
(September 13, 1936), 302-304.

"Duel without Pistols, " Collier's, CXXX (August 23,
1952), 13-15, 26ff.

"Easiest Way to Die, " Saturday Review, XLI (August
23, 1958), 12ff.

Foreword to Between Pacific Tides. Stanford Univ.
Press, 1948.
An offprint from the revised edition, issued August,
1948, of a work by Edward F. Ricketts and Jack
Calvin. Privately printed at the Stanford Univ. Press
by Nathan Van Patten.

Foreword to Burning Bright, a play in story form.
New York: Viking Press, 1950. pp. 9-13.

Foreword to Speeches of Adlai Stevenson, Ed. by
Richard Harrity. New York: Random House, 1952.
pp. 5-8.

"Gathering Knowledge, " in Treasure Chest, Ed. by
James D. Adams, New York: Dutton, 1946. p. 373.

"The GI's War......., " New York Herald Tribune
Weekly Book Review, May 18, 1947. p. 1.

"How to Fish in French, " Punch, XXII (August 25,
1954), 248-249.

"How to Tell Good Guys from Bad Guys, " Reporter,
XII (March 10, 1955), 42-44.
Also in The Art of the Essays, Ed. by Joseph Henry
Satin. New York: Crowell, 1958. pp. 357-362.

"I Go Back to Ireland, " Collier's, CXXXI (January 31,
1953), 48-50.
(Autobiographical)

"I Remember the Thirties, " in The Thirties; A Time
Remember, Ed. by Don Congdon. New York: Simon
& Schuster, 1962. pp. 23-36.

"In a Radio Broadcast Beamed," Saturday Review, XXXVIII (November 26, 1955), 8-9.

Introduction to The World of Li'l Abner by Al Capp. New York: Farrar, Strauss and Young, 1953.

"It Was Dark As Hell," in They Were There: The Story of World War II and How It Came About, Ed. by C. Riess. New York: Putnam's, 1944. pp. 584-585.

"Jalopies I cursed and Loved," Holiday, XVI (July, 1954), 44-45; 89-90.
Also in Ten Years of Holiday, Ed. by The Holiday editors. New York: Simon & Schuster, 1956. pp. 439-444.

"Joan in All of Us," Saturday Review, XXXIX (January 14, 1956), 17.

"Mail I've Seen," Saturday Review, XXXIX (August 4, 1956), 16.

"Madison Avenue and the Election," Saturday Review, XXXIX (March 31, 1956), 11.

"Making of a New Yorker," New York Times Magazine, February 1, 1953. VI, Pt. III, p. 26
February 22, 1953. VI, p. 4.
Also in Empire City: A Treasury of New York, Ed. by A. Klein. New York: Rinehart, 1955. pp. 469-475.

"Man with a Ski Nose," This Was Your War, Ed. by Frank Bookhauser. New York: Dell, 1963.

"Miracle Island of Paris," Holiday, XIX (February, 1956), 43.

"A Model T Named 'It'," Ford Times, XLV (July, 1953), 34-39. Also in High Gear, ed. by Evan Jones. New York: Bantam, 1955. pp. 64-66.

"More About Aristocracy," Saturday Review, XXXVIII (December 10, 1955), 11.

"My Short Novel," Wings, XXVI (October, 1953), 1-8. (Literary Guild Review)

Also in English Journal, XLIII (March, 1954), 147.
(Excerpt from Wings).

"My War with the Ospreys," Holiday, XXI (March,
1957), 72-73; 163-165.
Also in Essays Today 3, Ed. by M. Ludwig.
New York: Harcourt, Brace, 1958.

"Mystery of Life," in Treasure Chest, Ed. by James
Donald Adams. New York: Dutton, 1946. pp. 371-
372.

"The Novel Might Benefit By the Discipline and Terse-
ness of the Drama," Stage, XV (January, 1938),
50-51.

"On Learning Writing," in Writer's Yearbook, No. 34,
1963. Cincinnati: F. and W. Publishing Co., 1963.
p. 10.

"One American in Paris," in Holiday in France,
Selected and decorated by L. Bemelmans. Boston:
Houghton, Mifflin Co., 1957. p. 141.

"One More for Lady Luck," in Star Reporters and 34
of Their Story, Ed. by W. Greene. New York:
Random House, 1948. pp. 320-324.
(Dispatch to New York Herald Tribune from London,
1943.)

"Our Best, Our Fliers," New York Times Magazine,
November 22, 1942. pp. 16-17.

"Our Rigged Morality," Coronet, XLVII (March, 1960),
144-147.
Also in Fabulous Yesterdays, Ed. by Lewis W.
Gellenson. New York: Harper, 19??
(Steinbeck and Adlai Stevenson, an exchange of letters.)

"Over There," Ladies' Home Journal, LXI (February,
1944), 20-21.
Also in The Ladies' Home Treasury, Ed. by John
Mason Brown and the Editors of The Ladies' Home
Journal. New York: Simon & Schuster, 1956.

"A Plea to Teachers," National Education Association
Journal, XLIV (September, 1955), 359.

Also in Saturday Review, **XXXVIII** (April 30, 1955), 24.

"Poker for Keeps," in Masterpieces of War Reporting, Ed. by Louis L. Snyder. New York: Julius Messner, 1962. p. 314.

Preface to Story Writing, By Edith Ronald Mirrielees. New York: Viking Press, 1962. Viking (Compass C 111).

"A President. . . . Not a Candidate," Washington, D. C.: 1964 Democratic Convention Program Book Committee, 1964.

"A Primer on the 30's," Esquire, **CIII** (June, 1960), 85-93.

"Random Thoughts on Random Dogs," in Cold Noses and Warm Hearts. Englewood Cliffs, N. J.: Prentice-Hall, 1958. p. 1.

"Random Thoughts on Random Days," Saturday Review, **XXXVIII** (October 8, 1955), 11. Also in Saturday Review Treasury, Ed. by Saturday Review. New York: Simon & Schuster, 1957. pp. 529-531.

"Rationale," SHC. pp. 308-309.

"Robert Capa," Photography, **XXXV** (September, 1954), 48-53.

"Robert Capa," (an Appreciation by John Steinbeck) in Images of War by Robert Capa. New York: Grossman, 1964. p. 7. (Introduction to the book.)

"The Routine at a Bomber Station," in This War Your War, Ed. by Frank Bookhauser. New York: Dell, 1963. (#8798)

"The Secret Weapon We Were Afraid to Use," Collier's, **CXXXI** (January 10, 1953), 9-13. (Autobiographical)

"Some Thoughts on Juvenile Delinquency," Saturday

Review, XXXVIII (May 28, 1955), 22.

"The Soul and Guts of France, " Collier's, CXXX
(August 30, 1952), 26ff.

"Spivacks Beat the Odds; Condensed from The Journal
of American Medical Association in Reader's Digest,
LXXIII (October, 1958), 153-154.
See "Dedication. "

"The Stars Point To Shafter, " The Progressive Weekly,
December 24, 1938. n. p.

"Steinbeck's Voices of America, " Scholastic, LXV
(November 3, 1954), 15f.

"The Stevenson Spirit, " in The Faces of Five Decades,
Selected from Fifty Years of the New Republic,
1914-1964. Introduced by A. M. Schlesinger, Jr.
New York: Simon & Schuster, 1964. p. 332.

"Trade Wind: Predictions of Reviews East of Eden
Would Receive, " Saturday Review, XXXVII (February
27, 1954), 8.

"Troopship: Condensed from New York Herald Tribune."
Reader's Digest, XLIV (March, 1944), 67-70.

"Trust Your Luck, " Saturday Review, XL (January 12,
1957), 42-44.

Vanderbilt Clinic. New York: Presbyterian Hospital,
1947.
An illustrated brochure, with commentary by Steinbeck on the services of the Medical Center and its
clinics.
With Victor Keppler as photographer.
(Pamphlet)

"Vegetable War, " Saturday Review, XXXIX (July 21,
1956), 34-35.

"What Is The Real Paris?" Holiday, XVIII (December,
1955), 94.

"Women and Children in the U. S. S. R. , " Ladies' Home
Journal, LXV (February, 1948), 44-59.

21

"Work of W. F. Cody," Saturday Review of Literature, XXVIII (July 7, 1945), 18-19.

H. Newspaper Reports
Dispatches from The European War Theater appearing in The New York Herald Tribune, June 21 to December 10, 1943.

June 21(p.1); 22(p.1); 23(p.1); 24(p.1); 25(p.1); 26(p.1); 27(p.1); 28(p.1); 29(p.23); 30(p.23)

July 1(p.21); 2(p.17); 3(p.13); 4(p.7); 5(pp.1, 9); 6(p. 17); 7(p.23); 8(p.21); 9(p.15); 10(p.7); 11(p.14); 12 (p.15); 13(p.21); 14(p.21); 15(p.21); 16(p.13); 17 (p.7); 18(p.18); 19(p.13); 25(p.12); 26(p.17); 27(p.17); 28(p.17); 29(p.17); 30(p.13)

August 3(p.15); 4(p.17); 5(p.17); 6(p.13); 9(p.11); 10 (p.21); 12(p.17); 26(p.15); 27(p.13); 28(p.7); 29(p.10); 31(p.17)

September 1(p.21); 2(p.21); 3(p.17); 5(p.5); 17(p.3); 29(p.21)

October 1(p.21); 3(p.35); 4(p.13); 6(p.25); 8(p.17); 11(p.17); 12(p.21); 13(p.25); 14(p.25); 15(p.1); 18 (p.17); 19(p.21); 20(p.1); 21(p.1); 29(p.17)

November 1(p.17); 3(p.23); 5(p.15); 8(p.17); 15(p.17); 17(p.25); 19(p.21); 22(p.17); 24(p.17); 26(p.21)

December 1(p.23); 3(p.21); 6(p.21); 8(p.25); 10(p.25)

Reference taken from Peter Lisca's dissertation.)

"The Harvest Gypsies," San Francisco News, October 5-12, 1936.
A series of articles on migrant labor in California.

Chapter I.	October 5, 1936	(p. 3)
II.	" 6, "	(p. 3)
III.	" 7, "	(p. 6)
IV.	" 8, "	(p. 16)
V.	" 9, "	(p. 14)
VI.	" 10, "	(p. 14)
VII	" 11, "	(p. 8)

(Reference taken from Peter Lisca's dissertation.)

22

"Troopship: Condensed from New York Herald Tribune,"
Reader's Digest, XLIV (March, 1944), 67-70.

I. Verse
"Atropos: Study of a Very Feminine Obituary Editor,"
Stanford Lit, I (March, 1926), 95.
(Stanford Lit is not an abbreviation of Stanford
Literature.)

"Baubles," Monterey Beacon, I (January 5, 1935), 7.
(Amnesia Glasscock as pseudonym)

"Four Shades of Navy Blue," Monterey Beacon, I
(January 26, 1935), 12.
(Amnesia Glasscock as pseudonym)

"The Genius," Monterey Beacon, I (January 26, 1935),
12.
(Amnesia Glasscock as pseudonym)

"If Eddie Guest Had Written the Book of Job: Happy
Birthday," Stanford Lit, I (March, 1926), 94.

"If John A. Weaver Had Written Keats' Sonnet in the
American Language: On Looking at a New Book by
Harold Bell Wright," Stanford Lit, I (March, 1926),
94.

"Ivanhoe," Monterey Beacon, I (January 26, 1935), 12.
(Amnesia Glasscock as pseudonym)

"Mammy," Monterey Beacon, I (January 5, 1935), 7.
(Amnesia Glasscock as pseudonym)

"Thoughts on Seeing a Stevedore," Monterey Beacon, I
(January 26, 1935), 11.
(Amnesia Glasscock as pseudonym)

"To Carmel," Monterey Beacon, I (January 5, 1935), 7.
(Amnesia Glasscock as pseudonym)

"The Visitor," Monterey Beacon, I (January 5, 1935), 7.
(Amnesia Glasscock as pseudonym)

J. Collected Works
The Long Valley. New York: Viking Press, 1938.
Including the following short stories:

"The Chrysanthemums"
"The White Quail"
"Flight"
"The Snake"
"The Breakfast"
"The Raid"
"The Harness"
"The Vigilante"
"Johnny Bear"
"The Murder"
"St. Katy the Virgin"
Red Pony:
   The Gift
   The Great Mountain
   The Promise
"The Leader of the People"

See I. E.

The Portable Steinbeck, Ed. by Pascal Covici.
New York: Viking Press, 1943.
Enlarged editions, 1946 and 1958.

Contents:
I. Introduction by Lewis Garnett
II. Excerpts from: The Long Valley; The Pastures of
    Heaven; Tortilla Flat; In Dubious Battle; The
    Grapes of Wrath; The Sea of Cortez; The Moon
    is Down; Bombs Away; Cannery Row
III. Complete works:
    Of Mice and Men; The Red Pony; A Fragment
    (Breakfast); An uncollected story: How Edith
    McGillcuddy Met R. L. S.

The Red Pony. New York: Covici-Friedi, 1937.
I.   The Gift
II. The Great Mountains
III. The Promise (The 1945 ed. includes IV.   The
   Leader of the People.)
See I. E.

The Short Novels. Introduced by Joseph Henry Jackson.
New York: Viking Press, 1953.
Book Club Edition, 1963.
This includes:
Cannery Row; The Moon is Down, Of Mice and Men;
The Pearl; The Red Pony; and Tortilla Flat

London: Heinemann, 1954.
New edition: completely reset in 1963, with Tortilla
Flat newly copyrighted 1962 and The Red Pony in 1961.

The Steinbeck Omnibus, Ed. by Pascal Covici.
London: William Heinemann, 1950.
Includes long and representative passages or complete
stories from:
The LV; The Pastures of Heaven; Tortilla Flat; In
Dubious Battle; The Grapes of Wrath; Sea of Cortez;
The Moon is Down; and Bombs Away. In addition Of
Mice and Men and The Red Pony are given complete,
the latter including the 4th part, not published in the
original volume.

.....13 Great Short Stories From the Long Valley.
New York: Avon Book Co., 1943.

K. Letters
Bradley, Berton.
"A Letter of John Steinbeck," in Morgan Sails the
Caribbean. New York: Macmillan, 1934. pp. vii-
viii.
(Steinbeck gives his permission to the author to use
certain incidents from Cup of Gold.)

The First Watch. Ward Ritchie Press, 1947.
Steinbeck's humorous letter of thanks for the gift of
a watch.

"Izvestia published Steinbeck letter apologizing to Soviet
writers who were his hosts during 1963 visit for mix-
ing up over copies of his 1962 Nobel Prize speech
and mimeographing thank-you list he sent to them and
accidentally to others he had never met," New York
Times, August 30, 1964. p. 24.

John Steinbeck Replies. New York: Friends of
Democracy, Inc., 1940.
A letter written in reply to a request for a statement
about his ancestry, together with the letter originally
submitted by the Friends of Democracy.
A printed leaflet containing an exchange of letters between the author and Rev. L. M. Birkhead, national
director of the Friends of Democracy.

Stamford, Conn.: The Overbrook Press, 1940.

350 copies only.

"A Letter of Steinbeck, " in The Thinking Dog's Man.
By Ted Patrick.   New York: Random House, 1964.
Contains Steinbeck's letter used as introduction.

"A Letter on Criticism, " Corolado Quarterly, IV
(Autumn, 1955), 218-219.
Also in SHC. pp. 52-56.

"Letters to Alicia, " A series of letters addressed to
Alicia (Patterson Guggenheim), published in Newsday,
starting November 20, 1965.   Alicia is the late wife
of the editor and publisher of Newsday.
(Also in Sunday Bulletin of News and Views Section,
Philadelphia,)

"A Letter to Inmates of The Connecticut State Prison, "
Monthly Record, a monthly journal devoted to the
interests of the inmates.
(n. v.)   (June, 1938), n. p.

"Postscript from Steinbeck, " in SHC.   pp. 307-308.

"Steinbeck's Letter, " in Writers Take Sides.
New York: The League of American Writers, 1938.
(Letters about the war in Spain from 418 American
authors.)

"The Way It Seems to John Steinbeck, " Occident (Fall,
1936), n. p.

L. Speeches
"John Steinbeck's (Nobel Prize) Acceptance Speech, "
Vogue, CXLI (March 1, 1963), 16.

"Man's Hope: Steinbeck in Stockholm; Excerpt from His
Address, " Newsweek, LX (December 24, 1962), 67.

His Nobel Prize Acceptance Speech on December 10,
1962 quoted in Contemporary Authors, II.
Michigan: Gale Research Co. , 1963.   p. 184.
See II.

"Nobel Prize Acceptance Speech, " in Story, Issue 2,
Vol. XXXVI (March-April, 1963). New York: Story
Magazine, 1962.

26

"Nobel Prize Acceptance Speech," A Supplement to the
Book-of-the-Month Club News.
New York: Book-of-the-Month Club, 1962.
(4 page pamphlet)

"Speech Accepting the Nobel Prize for Literature,
Stockholm, December 10, 1962.
New York: Viking Press, 1962.
3,200 copies have been printed.

M. Excerpts From Steinbeck's Major Works
Bombs Away in Portable Steinbeck, Ed. by Pascal
Covici. New York: Viking Press, 1943.

Cannery Row in Portable Steinbeck.

"Life in the Great Tide Pool; Excerpt from Cannery
Row," in Book of the Sea, Ed. by A. C. Spectorsky.
New York: Appleton-Century-Crofts, 1954. pp.
450-451.

East of Eden:

"Writer's Credo; Excerpt from East of Eden," in
Reader's Digest, LXII (March, 1953), 130.

The Grapes of Wrath in Portable Steinbeck.

Chapter 13, 14, and 15 from The Grapes of Wrath in
The Literature of the United States, Ed. by W.
Blair, et al. Chicago: Scott, Foresman and Co.,
1949.

"The Okies," in The Great Depression, Ed. by David
A. Shannon. Englewood Cliffs, N. J.: Prentice-
Hall, 1964. pp. 68-71.

"Social 'World' of the Transients' Camp; Excerpt from
The Grapes of Wrath," in Outside Readings in Soci-
ology, Ed. by E. A. Schuler, et al. New York:
Crowell, 1952, pp. 170-174.

"Women Watch Their Men; Excerpt from The Grapes of
Wrath," in Treasure Chest, Ed. by James D. Adams,
New York: Dutton, 1946. pp. 374-375.

"The World of the Migratory Worker," Excerpt from

The Grapes of Wrath in Sociology Through Literature,
Ed. by Lewis A. Loser, New York: Prentice Hall,
1963.

"No Riders; Story Excerpt from The Grapes of Wrath,"
in Saturday Review, XIX (April, 1939), 13-14.

"Two for a Penny; Story Abridged from The Grapes of
Wrath," in Reader's Digest, XXXVII (August, 1940),
9-12.

In Dubious Battle in Portable Steinbeck.

The Log From the Sea of Cortez:

"Out of the Two Approaches; Excerpt from The Log
From the Sea of Cortez, in Writing From Experience,
Ed. by Richard A. Condon and B. O. Kurth. New
York: Harper, 1960. pp. 119-122.

The Long Valley

The Portable Steinbeck

The Moon is Down in Portable Steinbeck.

The Moon is Down in Reader's Digest, XL (June, 1942),
115-152. Abridged.

The Moon is Down: A Play in Two Parts, abridged in
The Best Plays in 1941-1942, Ed. by Robert B.
Mantle. New York: Dodd, Mead and Co., 1942.
pp. 72-108.

Of Mice and Men: A Play in Three Acts, abridged in
The Best Plays of 1937-1938, Ed. by Robert B.
Mantle. New York: Dodd, Mead and Co., 1938.
pp. 31-66.

Once There Was a War:

"Man with a Ski Nose; Excerpt from Once There Was a
War," in This Was Your War, Ed. by F. Brookhouser.
Garden City, N. Y.: Doubleday, 1960. pp. 431-433.

"The Routine at a Bomber Station; Excerpt from Once
There Was a War," in This Was Your War. pp.

256-258.

The Pastures of Heaven in Portable Steinbeck.

A Russian Journal:

"We can Only Think of Augustus Caesar; Excerpt from
A Russian Journal," in Treasury of Great Reporting:
Literature Under Pressure From the 16th Century
to our Own Time, Ed. by L. L. Syder and R. B.
Morris. New York: Simon & Schuster, 1949. pp.
711-713.

The Sea of Cortez in Portable Steinbeck.

"Easter Sunday," Sea of Cortez in The World's Best:
105 Greatest Living Authors, Ed. by Whit Burnett.
New York: Dial Press, 1950. pp. 61-76.
(Chapter 14 of The Log. "March 24, Easter Sunday.")

Tortilla Flat in Portable Steinbeck.

Travels with Charley in Reader's Digest, LXXXIV (June,
1964), 275-278f. Abridged.

"John Steinbeck's Travels With Charley in Search of
America," Excerpt in Americana, The American
Motors Magazine, I (November-December, 1965),
21-22.

Travels With Charley in Search of America, an Excerpt
in The Whole Wide World, A Treasury of Great
Travel Writings of our Time, Ed. by William Clifford.
New York: Crown, 1965, pp. 53-57.

N. Recordings
   Columbia, ML-4756. "The Snake," "Johnny Bear" from
   The Long Valley.
   Steinbeck reads his own short stories.
   (Reference taken from Warren G. French's John
   Steinbeck.)

O. Manuscripts
   A List of Steinbeck Manuscripts; Unpublished Letters by
   and to the Author, Documents and Special Collections
   Relating to Him
   (Materials are arranged by institution in which they

are currently held.)

1. American Academy of Arts and Letters
   633 West 155th Street
   New York, N. Y. 10032

   One-page handwritten critical appraisal of John O'Hara

   Seven letters to Miss Felicia Geffen, Assistant to the President of the Academy

   Thirteen letters to the author

   Two documents relating to the author: his nomination to the National Institute of Arts and Letters, and his nomination to the American Academy of Arts and Letters

2. The California State Library
   Sacramento, California

   Two author cards filled out by the author in June, 1935.

3. Cornell University Library
   Ithaca, N. Y. 14850

   Three ALS to Franklin Folsom, October 2, 1938? 1p. ; to George Jean Nathan, April 19, 1938, 1p. ; and to George Jean Nathan, May 23, 19??, 1p.

   One letter from Theodore Dreiser, January 24, 1940, 4p.

4. Harvard University
   The Houghton Library
   Cambridge, Mass. 02138

   T MSS: "The Days of Long Marsh"
   "East Third Street"
   "The Nail"
   "The Nymph and Isobel. "
   (Transcribed by Lawrence Clark Powell from the original; not to be published during the author's lifetime.)

   Twenty-one letters by the author:

ALS to William Needham, September 9, 1936

Seven ALS and APS to Lawrence Clark Powell, October, 1936-April 5, 1939 and n. d.

TLS to Roger W. Watkins, May 13, 1938

Three ALS to Alexander Woolcott, May 7, 1937-August 29, 1937

Miscellaneous newspaper clippings, offprints, bibliographical notes, etc., collected by Lawrence Clark Powell.

5. Indiana University Library
   Bloomington, Indiana

   One ALS to Upton Sinclair from Los Gatos, Calif., n. d.

   ALS from Los Gatos, Calif., April 3, 1934 (carbon copy).

6. The Library of Congress
   Manuscript Division
   Washington, D. C.   20540

   The Grapes of Wrath, TL with MS corrections. 751 p.

   The Grapes of Wrath, corrected proof sheets

   (Both were presented to the Library by the late Frank J. Hogan in 1941.)

   The Sea of Cortez in collaboration with Edward F. Ricketts, TS with MS corrections.   447 p., September 5, 1941

   The Sea of Cortez, corrected proof sheets and a typewritten bibliography, with related correspondence

   (The Sea of Cortez presented to the Library by Viking Press, March 18, 1943).

7. Louisiana State University
   Department of Archives and Manuscripts
   Baton Rouge, La. 70803

Two letters which mention the author:
TLS by Lyle Saxon to Judith Hyamas Douglas,
1943, 2 p., March 24, 1943 and June 1, 1943
(Three letters are in the Judith Hyamas Douglas
Papers, a collection of 578 items of the late Mrs.
Douglas (1875-1955).)

8. Mills College Library
Oakland, California 94613

ALS to Albert Bender, n.d., about 5 lines, in which
the author declines an invitation to see Mr. Bates

9. The Pierpont Morgan Library
33 East Thirty-sixth Street
New York, N. Y. 10016

One ALS by the author

"Address before the Swedish Academy on Receiving
the Nobel Prize for Literature":

Eight MS pages in pencil: p. 1, outline of
address; pp. 2-8 includes first and second draft
of the proposed speech

TS of early drafts of speech with MS corrections,
3 p. With three carbon copies, uncorrected

Three MS pages of part of third draft, with three
TS pages slightly corrected
With two carbon copies, uncorrected

Three four-page TS after the above

Five MS and corrected TS pages of the fifth draft

Final MS draft headed "Freeze it now. " 4 p.

TS of speech with MS slips added

Final TS of speech with MS slips added and TS
much corrected

TS of radio announcement made on the 25th of
October, 1962 by Dr. Anders Osterling, et al.
Printed two leaf pamphlets issued by the Book-of-

the-Month Club, "Nobel Prize Acceptance Speech by John Steinbeck"

"Short Reign of Pippin IV": The author's MS consisting of thirty autograph pages, 196 typewritten pages with autograph corrections and additions, and sixty-four uncorrected typewritten pages (c. 1957)

"The Winter of Our Discontent, " MS in pen and pencil on sheets of yellow pad paper. 1960-61. 356 p. (This item is in addition to the later typewritten MS with autograph corrections which was presented to the Library by Steinbeck in 1961.)

"The Winter of Our Discontent, " MS.

"Travels with Charley in Search of America, " MS.

(The last two items were presented by the author in 1961).

10. Museum of the City of New York
5th Avenue at 104th Street
New York, N. Y. 10029

"The Moon is Down" Mi MS, 102 p. (the play at the Martin Beck Theatre on April 7, 1942)

11. New York Public Library
Fifth Avenue and 42nd Street
New York, N. Y. 10018

"Tortilla Flat" MS foreword, 1937. 5 p. (MS and letters in the Berg Collection)

ALS to Whitfield Kane, February, 1950. 1 p., w.e. (in the Whitfield Kane Papers)

ALS to (John Mackenzie) Cory, September 14, 1953. 1 p. (in Miscellaneous Papers)

12. Stanford University Libraries
Stanford, California

TLS to Anne Hadden, February 8, 1935, 2 p.

ALS to Leon Gelber, August 15, 1940, 1 p.

13. Tulane University
Howard-Tilton Memorial Library
New Orleans, La.

ALS to Lyle Saxon, "New Orleans, January 6, 1964,"
2 p, Gwyn Steinbeck to Saxon, "June 22, 1943," 1 p;
"New York, October 1, 1943," 1 p.; and "Mexico
(City), March 8, 1944," 1 p.

14. University of California
The Bancroft Library
Berkeley, California 94720

Four folders containing:

A letter from the Cerveceria Cuanhtemoc in
Monterrey, Mexico, December 22, 1944; and a carbon of a release of rights, October 12, 1944

ALS to Joseph Fontenrose, February 2, 1949, 2 p.,
w. e. and 1-leaf TS; Also copy of prospectus of essay
by the latter, 2-leaves

TS of unpublished essay, with explanatory note.
Carbon, 2-leaves, TS, 1-leaf

In addition the Bancroft Library has the following:

Fifty-one letters from the author during the period
1930-50 (in the George S. Albee Papers), with a
letter, October 11, (1935) from Carol H. Steinbeck
and a postcard, c. September 20, (1951) from Elaine
S. Steinbeck

Thirty-five letters from the author during 1936-1948
(in the Joseph Henry Jackson Papers)

ALS from the author, March 23, 1959 (in the Gertrude
Alberton Papers)

ALS from the author, February 19, 1959 (in the Mark
Schorer Papers)

ALS from the author to Benjamin H. Lehman, c.1932,
TSS, 1-leaf (in the Rafe Book Room of the General
Library)

15. University of Colorado Library
    Boulder, Colorado 80304

    ALS to Paul Carter, February 2, 1955, 2 p., 48
    lines on legal size paper

16. University of Pennsylvania
    The Charles Patterson Van Pelt Library
    Philadelphia, Pa.

    Four letters from the author:
        To Theodore Dreiser, January 28, 1940, 1 p.
        To Burton Rascoe, January 25, 1935?, 1 p.;
        September 9, 1935, 1 p.; and January 12, 1936,
        1 p.

17. University of Southern California Library
    Los Angeles, California 90007

    ALS by the author to Karl Zamboni, a Los Angeles
    book dealer, January 2, 1935

18. The University of Texas
    Academic Center Library
    Austin, Texas

    Five ALS to Ben Abromson, n.d., 1 p.; n.d., 1 p.;
    n.d., 1 p.; n.d., 1 and 1/2 p.; and n.d., 1 p.

    ANS to Ben Abromson, July 22, 1941, 1 p.

    Two APS to Ben, "March 4, 1935"; and "October 16,
    1935"

    TLS to Ben, July 14, 1935, 1 p.

    List of names headed "Of Mice and Men", 3 p., with
    signed note to Ben on p. 3, n.d.

    ANS to Mrs. (John Stuart) Groves, "February 27,
    1956"

    TLS to Mabs (Gertrude Anderson), February 19, 1947,
    1 p.

    TL to Mabs and Max, December 1, 1947, 1 p.

TLS to Max, a note saying "Answered November 29, 1946), 1 p.

Three ALS to Max and Mabs, January 3, 1946, 1 p.; January 25, 19??, 1 p. ("January 28, 1950"); and n.d. ("April 21, 1946")

Telegram from the author to Gwyn Conger and Maxwell Anderson, June 22, 1949

Telegram to Maxwell Anderson, January 7, 19??

ALS to Mrs. (Francis Warren) Roberts, February 8, 1960, 1 p.

19. University of Virginia
    The Clifton Waller Barrett Library
    Charlottesville, Va.

"The Grapes of Wrath": AMS for The Grapes of Wrath in ink on 165 pages of blue-lined paper removed from a bound ledger (10" x 16")

The MS is untitled and is headed, "New Start/ Big Writing" (referring to the size of the handwriting)

(Acquired for the Clifton Waller Barrett Library by Mr. Barrett from John Howell Books of San Francisco in 1954. John Howell Books had acquired it from Steinbeck's former wife, Carol.)

"The Grapes of Wrath": Photocopy of TPS, December 17, 1960 to Warren R. Howell

ALS to Henry Moore, February or March, 1936

AMS, n.d., bearing note in hand of (Gene Salow) "added scene for picture version of "Of Mice and Men".....cut out of picture, 3 p.

Letters:

Fifteen ALS to Gene Salow, "August 19, 1949," 2 p., w.e.;

> October 11, 1949, 1 p., w.e.;
> "December 30, 1949," 1 p., w.e.;

January 25, (1950), w. e. ;
"February 8, 1950, " 2 p. , w. e. ;
"February 20, 1950, " 1 p. , w. e. ;
"March 30, 1950, " 1 p. , w. e. ;
"April 11, 1950, " 1 p. , w. e. ;
"August 15, (1950), 2 p. , w. e. ;
August 22, (1950), 1 p. , w. e. ;
September 14, (1950), 1 p. , w. e. ;
"October 21, 1950, " 1 p. , w. e. ;
November 2, (1950), 1 p. , w. e. ;
November 5, 1950 and November 17; (written in
two parts about a week apart), 4 p. , w. e. ;
January 27, (1951), 1 p. , w. e.

PS to Gene Salow, February 10, 1954

TLS to Gene Salow, November 9, 1962, 1 p. , w. e.

Photograph of post card, December 17, 1960 to John Howell

Newspaper picture of the author and his wife, Elaine, inscribed and initials by the author, n. d.

PS to Wilbur Needham, August 6, 1936, 2 p.

ALS to W. N. , April 4, (1934), 1 p. , w. e.

TLS to W. N. , "February 7, 1935, " 2 p. , w. e.

Two APS to W. N. , "January 3, 1936 and October 4, 1938"

TL to W. N. , "June 6, 1939, " 1 p. , w. e.

ALS to Merle Armitage, February 17, 1939

ALS to W. N. , "September 29, 1940, " 2 p.

TLS to M. A. , December 31, 1946, 1 p.

TLS to H. Kauti, February 16, 1953, 1 p.

TLS to M. A. , December 1, 1958, 1 p.

Two APS to W. N. , "n. d. , 1935 ?"; "February 12, 19 ? ?

Two ALS to W. N. from Manchester S. , Mexico D. F. , n. d. , 4 p. , w. e. ; and n. d. , written from Los Gatos, 1 p.

ALS to Docker, April 25, 19?? (Purchased on January 13, 1966)

20. Viking Press
625 Madison Avenue
New York, N. Y. 10022

Letters to Pascal Covici, 1937-1964

21. Yale University Libraries
New Haven, Conn. 06520

Two ALS and one TLS to Ben Abramson, one dated September 29 and others undated, from Los Gatos, 3 p.

TLS from a secretary to Fred B. Millet, April 28, 1937, from New York, N. Y. , 1-leaf, w. e.

Part II Secondary Material

A. Biography
Abramson, Ben. "John Steinbeck, " in Reading and
Collecting, I (December, 1936), 4-5; 18.
See II, B, 3.

"Assisting John Steinbeck, " Newsweek, XLVII (June,
1956), 56.
See II, B, 3.

"The Author John Steinbeck, " The Booklover's Answer,
No. 2 (November-December, 1962). Passim.

"Authors and Others, " Publisher's Weekly, CXXVIII
(July 27, 1935), 223.
See II, B, 3.

"Awards; Novel Prize in Literature, " Wilson Library
Bulletin, XXXVII (December, 1962), 321.

"Beach, Joseph Warren. "John Steinbeck: Journeyman
Artist, " in American Fiction, 1920-1940. N. Y. :
Macmillan, 1941. pp. 309-347.
Also in Tedlock & Wicker (eds.), SHC. pp. 80-91.
See II, B.

"Bennett, Robert. The Warth of John Steinbeck, or St.
John Goes to Church. Los Angeles: Albertson Press,
1939. (Pamphlet)
Also in The Monthly Record, (N. Y.) (June, 1950),
(n. p.).
See II, B.

"Bernie Byrnes Files Breach of Contract Suit Against
John Steinbeck, L. Milestone, & B. Meredith, "
N. Y. Times, February 24, 1948. p. 22.

Bidwell, Martin. "John Steinbeck: an Impression, "
Prairie Schooner, XII (Spring, 1938), 10-15.
See II, B, 3.

"Biggest Cinema Story Price," Time, XXXIX (May 11, 1942), 47. (The Moon is Down)
See II, B, 3.

"Biographical Notes," Scholastic, XLIII (December 6, 1943), 18; XLIV (April 24, 1944), 22.

"Biographical Sketch," Publishers' Weekly, CXXVIII (July 27, 1935), 223.

"Biographical Sketch," Saturday Review, XXX (February 15, 1947), 14.

"Biographical Sketch," Wilson Bulletin for Librarians, XI (March, 1937), 456.

"The Birth of Steinbeck," Wilson Library Bulletin, XIII (April, 1939), 540.

Blair, Walter, et al. (eds.) "John Steinbeck," in The Lit. of the United States. 3 vols. Chicago: Scott, Foresman & Co., 1953. pp. 783-784. Passim.
See II, B, 2.

Block, Maxine (ed.). "John Steinbeck," in Current Biography. N.Y.: H. W. Wilson, 1940. pp. 757-759.
See II, B, 2.

"Books into Films," Publishers' Weekly, CXLVII (January 13, 1945), 150.

Bregy, Katherine. "Of John Steinbeck," America, LXXI (August 19, 1944), 496-497.

"Business Journal," Time, LI (January 26, 1948), 58f.

"Buys 2 NYC. E. 78th St. Houses," New York Times, November 7, 1945, p. 30.

"Career," New York Times, February 11, 1940. IX, p. 4.

Champney, Freeman. "John Steinbeck," Californian," Antioch Review, VII (September, 1947), 345-362. Also in SHC. pp. 135-151.
See II, B, 3.

Covici, Pascal (ed.). "Introduction," in The Portable
Steinbeck, N.Y.: Viking Press, 1946. pp. vii-xxx.
See II, B, 3.

"Divorced," New York Times, March 19, 1943. p. 21.
(Carol Henning)

"Double Beating Views on American Soldiers, Reply to
the Editor of L'Unita," Time, LX (July, 1952), 48.

Du Bois, W. "Success Story," New York Times Book
Review, September 6, 1953. p. 8.

"East of Eden, a best-seller," Facts on File, XII
(October 31-November 6, 1952), 355.
See II, B, 3.

"East of Eden, a movie, was produced by Warner
Bros.," Facts on File, XV (April 7-13, 1955), 127.
See II, B, 3.

"Elected to the American Academy of Arts & Letters,"
Time, LII (December 6, 1948), 42.

"Elected American Arts & Letters Academy Member,"
New York Times, November 24, 1948. p. 44.

Ethridge, James M. (ed.). "Steinbeck," in Contem-
porary Authors A Bio-Bibliographical Guide to
Current Authors & Their Works, Detroit: Gale
Research Co., 1963. Vol. II p. 184.
See III.

"The Fiction Award," Saturday Review of Literature,
XXII (May 11, 1940), 5.

"Film Studios Bid for New Novel, Wayward Bus," New
York Times, November 3, 1946. II, p. 4.
See III, B, 3.

"La Follett Committee Investigation Based on The
Grapes of Wrath," Time, XXXIV (August 21, 1939),
10.
See II, B, 3.

Fontenrose, Joseph Eddy. John Steinbeck: An Introduction and Interpretation. New York: Barnes &

Noble, Inc., 1963. American Authors Critics Series, VIII. Ed. by John Mahoney.
See II, B, 1.

French, Warren. A Companion to the Grapes of Wrath. New York: Viking Press, 1963. pp. 51-92.
See II, B, 1.

French, Warren. John Steinbeck. New York: Twayne Publishers, Inc., 1961. U. S. Authors Series.
See II, B, 1.

French, Warren. Encyclopedia Americana. Vol. 25 N. Y.: Americana Corp., 1964. p. 612.
See II, B, 2.

Gannett, Lewis, "Introduction," in Portable Steinbeck. Edited by Pascal Covici. N. Y.: Viking Press, 1958. pp. vii-xviii.
See II, B, 2.

Gannett, Lewis. John Steinbeck, Personal & Bibliographical Notes. N. Y.: Viking Press, 1939, pamphlet. 15 pp.
See II, B, 1.

Gannett, Lewis. "John Steinbeck," in Preface to The Cup of Gold, N. Y.: Collier, 1936. pp. v-viii.
See II, B, 2; II, B, 3.

Gannett, Lewis. "Steinbeck," in Preface to Cup of Gold. N. Y.: Covici-Friede, 1936.
See II, B, 2; II, B, 3.

Geismar, Maxwell, David. "John Steinbeck," in his American Moderns: From Rebellion to Conformity. New York: Hill and Wang, 1958. pp. 151-156, 164-167.
See II, B, 2.

"Gets King Haakon's Liberty Cross," New York Times, November 16, 1946. p. 17.

"Gets Norwegian Award for Moon is Down," New York Times, January 21, 1947. p. 21.
See II, B, 3.

Gide, Andre. The Journals of Andre Gide. Tr. by
Justin O'Brien. N.Y.: Knopf, 1941. (September 27,
1940 & July 29, 1941.)
See II, B, 3.

"God and Man in Stockholm," America, CVIII (January
5, 1963), 4.

"Government Bans 182 Books Including Some By H. A.
Smith, John Steinbeck, H. Spring, & A. Murphy."
New York Times, January 21, 1956. VIII, p. 8.

"The Grapes Has First Birthday," Publishers' Weekly,
CXXXVII (April 13, 1940), 1493-1494. On The Grapes
of Wrath.
See II, B, 3.

"The Grapes of War; Steinbeck Prose From England,"
Newsweek, XXII (July 5, 1943), 94-96.
See II, B, 3.

"The Grapes of Wrath: Association of Farmers of Kern
County Seeks California Ban," New York Times,
August 23, 1939. p. 17.
See II, B, 3.

"The Grapes of Wrath Banned By Buffalo Library,"
Publishers' Weekly, CXXXVI (August 12, 1930), 453.
See II, B, 3.

"The Grapes of Wrath Banned in Kansas City," New
York Times, August 19, 1939. p. 8.
See II, B, 3.

"The Grapes of Wrath Consigned to Flames By Library
Board of East St. Louis, Illinois," Publishers'
Weekly, CXXXVI (November 25, 1939), 1994.
See II, B, 3.

"The Grapes of Wrath: East St. Louis Library Orders
Copies of The Grapes of Wrath Burned," New York
Times, November 15, 1939. p. 21.
See II, B, 3.

"The Grapes of Wrath Gets New Sales Stimulus,"
Publishers' Weekly, CXXXVI (December 30, 1939),
2320.

See II, B, 3.

"The Grapes of Wrath: He gives Pulitzer Prize Checks to R. Lovejoy for Literary Career, " New York Times, June 16, 1940. p. 3.
See II, B, 3.

"The Grapes of Wrath: He Wins American Booksellers Association Award, " New York Times, February 14, 1940. p. 19.
See II, B, 3.

"The Grapes of Wrath: He Winds Pulitzer Prize, " New York Times, May 7, 1940. p. 1.
See II, B, 3.

"The Grapes of Wrath: He Wins Social Work Today (Pub.) Award, " New York Times, April 2, 1940. p. 18.
See II, B, 3.

"The Grapes of Wrath: Mrs. F. D. Roosevelt Holds He Did Not Exaggerate, " New York Times, April 3, 1940. p. 25.
See II, B, 3.

"The Grapes of Wrath: Mrs. Roosevelt Comments on the Book, " New York Times, December 8, 1939. p. 16.
See II, B, 3.

"The Grapes of Wrath: Praised by Pearl Buck, " New York Times, November 30, 1939. p. 18.
See II, B, 3.

"The Grapes of Wrath: Screen Rights Sold, " New York Times, April 21, 1939. p. 21.
See II, B, 3.

"The Grapes of Wrath To Be Published, " New York Times, January 11, 1943. p. 2.
See II, B, 3.

"The Grapes of Wrath: To Collaborate with H. Kleine on Film Production, " New York Times, April 7, 1940. IX, p. 5.
See II, B, 3.

Hartrangt, Marshall V. Grapes of Gladness. Los
    Angeles: De Vorss & Co., 1939.
    See II, B, 1; II, B, 3.

Hart, James D. (ed.) "Steinbeck" in The Oxford Com-
    panion to American Literature. N.Y.: Oxford U.
    Pr., 1956. pp. 722-723.
    See II, B, 2.

"Has Eye Surgery," New York Times, June 25, 1962.
    p. 11.

His Nobel Prize Acceptance Speech on December 10,
    1962 Quoted in Contemporary Authors, Michigan:
    Gale Research Co., 1963. Vol II, p. 184.
    See I, L.

"Hurt in Apartment Mishap," New York Times, May
    16, 1947. 21.

Herzberg, Max J. and the Staff of The Thomas Y.
    Crowell Co. (eds.) "John Ernst Steinbeck," in The
    Reader's Encyclopedia of American Literature. N.Y.:
    Crowell, 1962. pp. 1079-1080.
    See II, B, 2.

Hutchens, J. K. "On an Author," New York Herald
    Tribune Book Review, September 21, 1952. p. 2.

Hyman, Stanley E. "John Steinbeck & The Nobel Prize,"
    New Leader, XLV (December 10, 1962), 10-11.

"Interview with a Best-Selling Author ᴸ John Stein-
    beck," Cosmopolitan, CXXII (April, 1947), 18, 123f.

"It Started in a Garden," Time, LX (September 22,
    1952), 110.

"Izvestia pub. J. Steinbeck Letter apologizing to Soviet
    Writers who were his hosts during 1963 visit for
    mix up over copies of his 1962 Nobel Prize speech
    & mimeographed thank-you list he sent to them &
    accidentally to others he had never met," New York
    Times, August 30, 1964. p. 24.

Jackson, Joseph Henry. "John Steinbeck, a Portrait,"
    Saturday Review of Literature, XVI (September 25,

1937), 11-12, 18.

Jackson, Joseph Henry. "Steinbeck," in Introduction to The Grapes of Wrath. N. Y.: Limited Edition Club & Heritage Press, 1940.
See II, B, 2; II, B, 3.

Jackson, Joseph Henry. "Steinbeck," in Introduction to Of Mice & Men. N. Y.: Random House, Modern Library, 1937.
See II, B, 2; II, B, 3.

Jackson, Joseph Henry. "John Steinbeck," in the preface to The Short Novels of John Steinbeck. N. Y.: Viking Press, 1903. pp. vii-xv.
See II, B, 2.

Jackson, Joseph Henry. Why Steinbeck Wrote The Grapes of Wrath. N. Y.: Limited Editions Club, 1940.
See II, B, 1; II, B, 3.

"John Steinbeck," Wilson Library Bulletin, XI (March, 1937), 456.

"John Steinbeck & Others Named Hon. Consultants in American Literature," New York Times, May 29, 1963. p. 40.

"John Steinbeck Charges USSR Fears Truth Above All Else," New York Times, June 27, 1952. p. 2.

"John Steinbeck Gets Press Medal of Freedom," New York Times, September 15, 1964. p. 15.

"John Steinbeck Hires Convention Leg Man," Editor & Publisher, LXXXIX (June 16, 1956), 10.

"John Steinbeck in USSR Under Cultural Program: S. Moscow," New York Times, October 22, 1963. p. 34.

"John Steinbeck, Made National Institute of Arts & Letters Member," New York Times, January 19, 1939. p. 15.

"John Steinbeck, One of The Kennedy Library Trustees," New York Times, January 14, 1964. p. 17.

"John Steinbeck, Special Guest, " New York Times,
September 3, 1947. p. 4; September 9, 1957. p. 3

"John Steinbeck To Continue in Journalism, " Editor and
Publisher, XC (April 27, 1957), 124.

"John Steinbeck To Get U. S. Medal of Freedom, " New
York Times, July 4, 1964. p. 1.

"John Steinbeck To Mexico City Literary Adaptations,
Actors Theatre, " New York Times, August 19, 1948.
p. 42.

"John Steinbeck Wins Back Rights to His Novel,
Cannery Row from Producer B. Bryants, " New York
Times, October 27, 1949. p. 38.
See II, B, 3.

"John Steinbeck Wins 1962 Nobel Prize for Literature, "
Publishers' Weekly CLXXXII (November 5, 1962),
20-21.

"Joins New York Herald Tribune Syndicate, " Time,
XLI (May 3, 1943), 49.

Kalb, Bernard. "The Author, " Saturday Review, XXXV
(September 20, 1952), 11.

Kalb, Bernard. "Biographical Note, " Saturday Review,
XXXV (September 20, 1952), 11.

Kunitz, Stanley J. (ed.) "John Steinbeck, " in Twentieth
Century Authors: A Biographical Dictionary of
Modern Literature. 1st Supplement. N. Y.: H. W.
Wilson, 1955 pp. 954-955. 1338-1339; 1942 ed

"Letter on the Ban of The Grapes of Wrath, " New York
Times, November 17, 1939. p. 20.
See II, B, 3.

Lisca, Peter, "The Art of John Steinbeck: An Analysis
and Interpretation of Its Development. " Unpublished
Ph. D. dissertation, University of Wisconsin, 1955.
Also in Dissertation Abstracts, XVI (1956), 965.
See II, B, 1.

Lisca, Peter. "John Ernst Steinbeck, " Collier's

Encyclopedia, 1964. XXI, p. 518.
See II, B, 2.

Lisca, Peter. "John Ernst Steinbeck, " Encyclopedia
Britannica. 1964. XXI, p. 377.
See II, B, 2.

Lisca, Peter. The Wide World of John Steinbeck.
New Brunswick, N. J.: Rutgers University Press,
1958.
See II, B, 1.

"The Literary Life: Impersonated, " Time, XL (August
17, 1942), 62.

Magill, Frank N. (ed.) "John Steinbeck, " in Cyclopedia
of World Authors. N. Y.: Salem Press, 1958, pp.
1017-1019.
See II, B, 2.

"Making of a New Yorker, " New York Times Magazine,
February 1, 1953. VI, Pt. III, p. 26; February 22,
1953. VI, p. 4. Autobiography.
Also in Empire City: A Treasury of New York Ed.
by A. Klein. N. Y.: Rinehart, 1955. pp. 469-475.
See III, B.

"Married, " Time, XLI (April 5, 1943), 76. (Gwyn
Conger)

"Medals of Freedom: John Steinbeck President Johnson
gave Medals of Freedom, the highest civilian honor
a President can vest on to 25 men & 5 women on
September 14, 1964. " Facts on File, XXIV (October 1-7, 1964), 335.

Millett, Fred B. "John Steinbeck, " in Contemporary
American Authors: A Critical Survey & 219 Bio-
Bibliographies. N. Y.: Harcourt, Brace & Co.,
1944. pp. 50; 596-597.
See II, B, 2.

Miron, George Thomas. The Truth About John Steinbeck & the Migrants. Los Angeles: Haynes Corp.,
1939.
See II, B, 1; II, B, 3.

"Mrs. Roosevelt Comment on The Grapes of Wrath,"
Time, XXXV (April 15, 1940), 17.
See II, B, 3.

"The Moon is Down Opens in Stockholm," Time, XLI
(April 19, 1943), 42.
See II, B, 3.

Moore, Harry Thornton. The Novels of John Stein-
beck: A First Critical Study. Chicago: Normandie
House, 1939.
See II, B, 1.

"More Wrath: Phony Pathos in Writings Flayed (Letter),"
Time, XXXV (March 25, 1940), 14.
See II, B, 3.

Moritz, Charles (ed.). "John Steinbeck," in Current
Biography. N.Y.: H. W. Wilson, 1940. pp. 757-759.
See II, B, 2.

"New York Censors Ban The Forgotten Village," Time,
XXXVIII (September 1, 1941), 54.
See II, B, 3.

"New York Herald Tribune Article on Visit to USSR
Criticized by Izvestia," New York Times, March 18,
1948. p. 14.

"New York Times and New York Herald Tribune Con-
flicting Reviews Cited in State Department Broadcast
to USSR," New York Times, February 18, 1947.
p. 18; February 19, 1947. p. 24.

Nichols, L. "Talk With John Steinbeck," New York
Times Book Review, September 28, 1952. p. 30.

"Nobel Prize Presented," Facts on File, XXII (December 20-26, 1962), 466.

"Of Mice and Men (Play) Receives Critics' Award,"
Time XXXI (April 25, 1938), 39.
See II, B, 3.

"Of Mice and Men (Play): Steinbeck Interviewed," New
York Times, December 5, 1937. p. 7.
See II, B, 3.

"Of Mice and Men (Play) Wins N. Y. Drama Critics
Circle Award, " New York Times, April 19, 1938.
p. 23.
See II, B, 3.

"Old Steinbeck, " Newsweek, LVII (June 26, 1961), 96.

Olson, Clarence E. "Fame Revisited: Nobel Award Has
Interrupted Steinbeck's Pursuit of Privacy, " St.
Louis Post Dispatch (Sunday Pictures), December 2,
1962. pp. 56-59.

"On Ernie Pyle as War Correspondent, " Time XLIV
(July 17, 1944), 65.

"Organization of World Video, " Time, LII (July 19,
1948), 65.

"Organizes World Video to Produce T. V. Shows:
Comment, " Time, LII (July 19, 1948), 65.

"Original Typescript of Book, The Grapes of Wrath
given to The Library of Congress, " New York Times,
December 25, 1941. p. 31.
See II, B, 3.

"Our Man in Helsinki, " New Yorker, XXXIX (November 9, 1963), 43-45.

"PEN Am. Center Invites 6 USSR Writers to Visit
U. S. : Invitation Sent By J. Steinbeck & E. Albee, "
New York Times, June 8, 1964. p. 26.

"Pipe Dream, By R. Rodgers and O. Hammerstein
II; John Steinbeck on His Novel Sweet Thursday from
Which Musical Was Adapted, " New York Times,
November 27, 1955. II, p. 1; December 11, 1955.
II, p. 1.
See II, B, 3.

"Pipe Dream, A Musical Comedy By Oscar Hammer-
stein II (Book & Lyrics) and Richard Rodgers (Music)
Based on John Steinbeck's novel, Sweet Thursday
Was Produced, " Facts on File, XV (December 1-7,
1955), 403.
See II, B, 3.

"Plush Stuff, " Newsweek, XLII (October 19, 1953), 114.

"Portrait, " Newsweek, XXXI (February 9, 1948), 76.

"Portrait of John Steinbeck, " New York Times, April 19, 1938. p. 23.

Powell, Lawrence Clark. "Birth of Steinbeck, " Wilson Bulletin for Librarians, XIII (April, 1939), 540.

"President and Mrs. Johnson Go by Helicopter to Camp David for Weekend; among Guests are Mr. and Mrs. John Steinbeck, " New York Times, July 18, 1965. I, p. 27.

"Pulitzer Award, " Scholastic, XXXVI (May 20, 1940), 28.

"Pulitzer Fiction Awards, " Saturday Review of Literature, XXII (May 11, 1940), 5f.

"Pulitzer Prize Recipient, " Time, XXXV (May 13, 1940), 77.

"R. Lardner, Jr. Banned By Film Company for Congressional Contempt Changes, Will Produce Film with John Steinbeck & B. Meredith, " New York Times, June 11, 1948. p. 27.

Roane, Margaret C. "John Steinbeck As A Spokesman for the Mentally Retarded, " Wisconsin Studies in Contemporary Literature, V (Summer, 1964), 127-132.

Robin, A. "Living Legends, " Today's Health, XLI (April, 1963), 5.

Sartre, Jean-Paul. "American Novelists in French Eyes, " Atlantic, CLXXVIII (August, 1946), 114-118.

"S. Bischoff Acquires Screen Rights to Book, Cup of Gold, " New York Times, December 16, 1945. II, p. 5.
See II, B, 3.

"Scandinavian Trip, " Time, XLVIII (November 11, 1946), 49.

Scherman, David E. & Redlich, Rosemarie. Literary
America: A Chronicle of American Writers from
1607-1952 with 173 Photographs of the American
Scene That Inspired Them. N. Y. : Dodd, Mead &
Co. , 1952. pp. 166-167. ("Route 66" from The
Grapes of Wrath.)

Singleton, R. H. (ed.) Two and Twenty, A Collection of
Short Stories. N. Y. : St. Martin's Press, 1962.
pp. 236-238 contain bio-bibliographical information.
See III

"Sixth American Writer to Win The Nobel Prize for
Literature, " Illustrated London News, CCXLI
(November 3, 1962), 715.

Slochower, Harry. "John Dos Passos & John Steinbeck,
Contrasting Notions of the Communal Personality, "
Bydcliffe Afternoons. Edited by C. E. Jones.
Woodstone, N. Y. : Overlook Press, 1940. pp. 11, 21.

Slochower, Harry. "Towards a Communal Personality, "
in No Voice is Wholly Lost. London: Dobson, 1946.
pp. 242-248.

"Steinbeck, " New York Herald Tribune, October 26,
1962. p. 41.

"Steinbeck, " New York Times, October 26, 1962. p. 1
& Passim.

"Steinbeck, " Newsweek, LX (November 5, 1962), 65.

"Steinbeck, " in Who's Who in America, 1962-1963
XXXII. Chicago: Marquis-Who's Who, 1963.

"Steinbeck as a Columnist of Long Island's Newsday. "
Time, LXXXVI (December 3, 1965), p. 68.

"Steinbeck Boom, " Wilson Bulletin for Librarians, XIII
(May, 1939), 640.

"Steinbeck: Critical Thorns and a Nobel Laurel, " Newsweek, LX (November 5, 1962), 65.

"Steinbeck Inflation, " Time, XXX (October 11, 1937), 79.

"Steinbeck Interviewed, " New York Times, September 28, 1958. VII, p. 30.

"Steinbeck narrates The Gift of the Magi, a Screenplay by Walter Bullock, " Facts on File, XII (October 31 - November 6, 1962), 355.

"Steinbeck Protests Barghoorn Arrest, " Facts on File, XXIII (November 14-20, 1963), 401.

"Steinbeck's The Wayward Bus Was Listed As an Obscene Book By The House Select Committee on Current Pornographic Materials in Washington, " Facts on File, XII (December 5-11, 1952), 397.
See II, B, 3.

"Steinbeck Visits Roosevelt, " New York Times, September 13, 1940. p. 10.

"Steinbeck Wins Nobel Prize, " Facts on File, XXII (November 1-7, 1962), 396.

The Swedish Academy & The Nobel Prizes: Its Official Statement Quoted in Contemporary Authors, Detroit: Michigan Gale Research Co., 1963. Vol. II, p. 184.

Taylor, Walter Fuller. "John Steinbeck, " in The Story of American Letters. Chicago: Henry Regnery, 1956. pp. 457-460.

Tedlock, Ernest W., Jr. and C. V. Wicker (eds.) Steinbeck and His Critics: A Record of Twenty-Five Years. Albuquerque: University of New Mexico Press, 1957.
See II, B, 1.

"Three New Plays Set, Moscow, Based on Works by Americans, John Steinbeck, J. Baldwin, & A. Mann," New York Times, September 14, 1964. p. 41.

"A Trip to Israel & His Forthcoming book, America and the Americans, " Time, LXXXVII (February 11, 1966), 41.

(Tsygankov, Veniamin.) "Steinbeck Play Praised, " New York Times, November 15, 1963. p. 5.

"U. S. : John Steinbeck Says Youth Lack Aims & Suffers From War Fears and Anxiety in USSR, " New York Times, October 19, 1963. p. 17.

Van Doren, Carol Clinton. "Steinbeck, " in Introduction to The Grapes of Wrath. Cleveland: World Publishing Co. , 1947.
See II, B, 3.

Van Gelder, Robert. "Interview with a Best-Selling Author John Steinbeck, " Cosmopolitan, CXXII (April, 1947), 18, 123f. Reprint from Writers & Writing. N. Y. : Scribner's, 1946.

"Venice International Biennial John Steinbeck Opens Exhibit of 65 Famous American Paintings, " New York Times, June 11, 1952. p. 36.

"Vestal High School, Vestal, N. Y. has faculty and students defy Harold C. May, the President of the Board of Education & put Steinbeck's The Grapes of Wrath on sale despite the board action. " New York Times, March 28, 1965. p. 76.
See II, B, 3.

Video V. Housework, " Time, LII (July 19, 1948), 65.

"Viewed As Nobel Literature Award Candidate, " New York Times, November 8, 1945. p. 6.

"Viking Portable Library Steinbeck Selected By P. Covici, " New York Times, August 22, 1943. VII, p. 6.

"The Viking Press Buys Contract, Orders for The Long Valley Earnings, " Time, XXXII (August 29, 1938), 47.
See II, B, 3.

"The Viking Press to Publish His Books, " New York Times, August 16, 1938. p. 17.

"Viva Zapata! Story of the Mexican Indian leader Emiliano Zapata, a screenplay By John Steinbeck, " Facts on File, XII (February 22-28, 1952), 67.
See II, B, 3.

"Voices of Author's Recordings," Life, XXXV (October 12, 1953), 132.

Warfel, Harry Redcay. "John Steinbeck," in American Novelists of Today, N. Y.: American Book Co., 1951, pp. 403-405.

Watt, Frank William. John Steinbeck, London: Oliver & Boyd, 1962. Writers & Critics Series, Ed. by A. Norman Jeffares. Also Evergreen Pilot EP 13 N. Y.: Grove Press, 1962.
See II, B, 1.

"The Wayward Bus," Facts on File, XVII (June 27 - July 3, 1963), 216.
See II, B, 3.

"Weds E. A. Scott," New York Times, December 29, 1950. p. 14.

"Weds G. Conger," New York Times, March 30, 1943. p. 23.

"Wife Gets Divorce," New York Times, March 13, 1942. p. 12. (Carol Henning.)

"Wife Gwyn Conger in Reno for Divorce; Dinner Partner Commits Suicide;" Time, LII (November 8, 1948), 44.

"Wins '62 Nobel Lit. Prize," New York Times, October 26, 1962. pp. 1; 12; 30; December 9, 1962. VII, p. 4; December 11, 1962. p. 3.

Witham, W. Tasker. "John Steinbeck," in Panorama of American Literature. N. Y.: Ungar, 1947. pp. 340-345.
See II, B, 2.

"Wrapped & Shellacked; Nobel Prize for Literature," Time, LXXX (November 2, 1962), 41-42.

"Writing for Short-Wave Broadcast to Soldiers," Time, XXXIX (May 18, 1942), 54.

"Wrote Story of Lifeboat," Time, XLIII (January 31, 1944), 94.

See II, B, 3.

Young, Stark. "Drama Critics Circle Award, " New
Republic, XCIV (May 4, 1938), 396. (On Of Mice
and Men.)

B. Criticism
1. Critical Books, Pamphlets, and Unpublished Theses
and Dissertations

Alexander, Charlotte. John Steinbeck's The Grapes of
Wrath. New York: Monarch Press, 1965.
Monarch Notes and Study Guides Series 692-4.

Bennett, Robert. The Wrath of John Steinbeck, or St.
John Goes to Church. Los Angeles: Albertson Press,
1939. (Pamphlet)
Also in The Monthly Record, n. v. (June, 1950),
n. p.
See II, A. ; II, B, 3.

Brown, Daniel. "Natural Men and Women in the Fiction
of John Steinbeck. " Unpublished Master's Thesis,
Kent State University, 1961.

Carey, Gary. The Grapes of Wrath by John Steinbeck:
Notes. Lincoln, Nebraska: Bethany Press, 1965.
73 pp.

Casimir, Louis J. , Jr. "Human Emotion and the Early
Novels of John Steinbeck, " Unpublished Ph. d.
dissertation, The University of Oklahoma, 1965.

Contents:
I.   The Problem; the Novels; the Criticism
II.   The Pastures of Heaven: There Are Serpents
        in Paradise.
III.   Tortilla Flat: A Funny Story But Not Pleasant
        to Laugh At.
IV.   In Dubious Battle: True Wars Are Never Won.
V.   Of Mice and Men: St. George and the Reluc-
        tant Dragon
VI.   The Red Pony and the Black Stallion: The
        Love and Death in the American Bildungs-
        roman
VII.   The Grapes of Wrath: They Just Kept Rolling
        Along

Cooperman, Stanley. Review and Notes and Study
Guide to Steinbeck. New York: Monarch Press, 1964.
(Monarch Review Notes and Study Guide Series 647)

Fontenrose, Joseph Eddy. John Steinbeck: An Intro-
duction and Interpretation. New York: Barnes and
Noble, Inc., 1963. American Authors and Critics
Series, VIII., Ed. by John Mahoney.
See II, B, 3.

Contents:
Chronology
I.   Biographical Introduction
II.   The First Novels
III.   The Pastures of Heaven
IV.   Tortilla Flat
V.   Torgas Valley and Long Valley
VI.   The Grapes of Wrath
VII.   Sea of Cortez
VIII.   The Moralities
IX.   East of Eden and After
X.   Conclusion
        Bibliography

Freel, Eugene L. "A Comparative Study Between
Certain Concepts and Principles of Modern Psychology
and the Main Writings of John Steinbeck." Unpublished Ph.d. dissertation, New York University,
1946.
Also in Microfilm Abstracts, VII (1947), 124. New
York University.

French, Warren G. (ed.). A Companion to The Grapes
of Wrath. New York: Viking Press, 1963.
See II, B, 3.

_____. "How Has The Grapes of Wrath Been
Received Abroad?" in French (ed.), A Companion
to The Grapes of Wrath. pp. 145-152.

_____. "How Was The Grapes of Wrath
Received at Home?" in French (ed.), pp. 105-111.

_____. "Is The Grapes of Wrath Art of
Propaganda?" in French (ed.), pp. 191-199.

_____. "Is the Movie Like the Book?" in

57

French (ed.), pp. 163-165.

_____. "Was The Grapes of Wrath Answered?"
in French (ed.), pp. 133-137.

_____. "What Became of the Joads?" in
French (ed.), pp. 93-101.

_____. "What Did John Steinbeck Know about
the 'Okies'?" in French (ed.), pp. 51-92.

French, Warren G. John Steinbeck. New York: Twayne
Publishers, Inc., 1961. U. S. Authors Series.
See II, B, 3.

Contents:
Chronology
1.   The Man Behind the Books
2.   Gatsby Sails the Caribbean
3.   Resurveying the Pastures of Heaven
4.   Ways Out of the Wasteland
5.   Morte d'Malory
6.   Parsifal's Last Stand
7.   End of a Dream
8.   Adventures in the Long Valley
9.   The Education of the Heart
10.   Steinbeck Goes to War
11.   The Intricate Music of Cannery Row
12.   The Defective Pearl
13.   The Lean Years
14.   Mr. Steinbeck Goes to Town
        Notes and References
        Selected Bibliography

Gannett, Lewis. John Steinbeck, Personal and Bibliographical Notes. New York: Viking Press, 1939.
See II, B, 3; III.

Goethals, Thomas R. The Grapes of Wrath: A
Critical Commentary. New York: R. D. M. Corpora-
tion, 1963.
See II, B, 3.

Hartrangt, Marshall V. Grapes of Gladness. Los
Angeles: De Vorss and Co., 1939.
(California's refreshing and inspiring answer to
Steinbeck's Grapes of Wrath, with extracts from

the reviews of The Grapes of Wrath by Burton
Rascoe, John D. Barry, and Thomas W. McMannus.
See II, B, 3.

Jackson, Joseph Henry. Why Steinbeck Wrote 'The
Grapes of Wrath'. New York: Limited Editions
Club, 1940.
See II, B, 3.

Kauth, Priscilla Jane. "Hemingway, Steinbeck, Warren,
Faulkner: The Sense of the Past." Unpublished
Master's Thesis, Stetson University, 1962.

Kontos, Peter G. "The Influence of Marxism on
Novels of Social Protest: 1930-1939," Unpublished
Master's Thesis, Kent State University, 1965.
"John Steinbeck," pp. 69-84.

Levant, Howard Stanley. "A Critical Study of the
Longer Fiction of John Steinbeck." Unpublished Ph. d.
dissertation, Cornell University, 1962.

Liedloff, Helmut. Steinbeck in German Translational
Practices. Southern Illinois University
Monographs, Humanities Series, No. 1.
Carbondale and Edwardsville: Southern Illinois
University, 1965.

Lisca, Peter. "The Art of John Steinbeck: An Analysis
and Interpretation of Its Development." Unpublished
Ph. D. dissertation, University of Wisconsin, 1955.
Also in Dissertation Abstracts, XVI (1956), 965.
See II, B, 3.

_____. The Wide World of John Steinbeck.
New Brunswick, N. J.: Rutgers University Press,
1958.
See II, B, 3; III.

Contents:
1.   Introduction: The Failure of Criticism
2.   Cup of Gold
3.   To a God Unknown
4.   The Pastures of Heaven
5.   Tortilla Flat
6.   The Long Valley
7.   In Dubious Battle

8.   Of Mice and Men
9.   The Grapes of Wrath
10.   Sea of Cortez, War Writings, The Moon is Down
11.   Cannery Row
12.   The Pearl
13.   The Wayward Bus
14.   Burning Bright
15.   East of Eden
16.   Sweet Thursday, The Short Reign of Pippin, IV, Some Conclusion
Notes; Checklist of Steinbeck's Published Work; Index.

Marks, Lester Jay. "A Study of Thematic Continuity in the Novels of John Steinbeck," Unpublished Ph.d. dissertation, Syracuse University, 1961.
Also in Dissertation Abstracts, XXII (1961), 4351.

Miron, George Thomas. The Truth About John Steinbeck and the Migrants. Los Angeles: Haynes Corp., 1939.

Monarch Review Notes and Study Guide Series
    See Alexander, Charlotte
    Cooperman, Stanley
    and
    Schwerner, Armand.

Moore, Harry Thornton. The Novels of John Steinbeck: A First Critical Study. Chicago: Normandie House, 1939.

Contents:
The Novels: A First Study
A Biographical Sketch
A Bibliographical Check-list
A Note Concerning the Map
See II, B, 3.

Schwerner, Armand. John Steinbeck's The Red Pony and The Pearl. New York: Monarch Press, 1965.
(Monarch Notes and Study Guide Series, 694-0)

_____. John Steinbeck's Mice and Men. New York: Monarch Press, 1965.
(Monarch Notes and Study Guide Series, 693-2.)

Taylor, Horace Platt, Jr. "The Biological Naturalism
of John Steinbeck." Unpublished Master's Thesis,
Stetson University, 1955.

_____. "The Biological Naturalism of John
Steinbeck." Unpublished Ph. d. dissertation, Louisiana
State University, 1962.
Also in Dissertation Abstracts, XXII (April, 1962),
3674.

Tedlock, Ernest W., Jr., and Wicker, C. V. (eds.).
Steinbeck and His Critics: A Record of Twenty-Five
Years. Alberquerque: University of New Mexico
Press, 1957.

Contents:
1.   Man and Career: Articles by Peter Lisca;
      Lewis Gannett; John Steinbeck
2.   Steinbeck on Criticism: 3 articles by Stein-
      beck
3.   Artist and Thinker: Articles by Burton
      Rascoe; F. J. Carpenter; J. W. Beach; L.
      R. Gibbs; E. B. Burgnm; J. S. Kennedy;
      F. Champney; S. E. Hyman; W. O. Ross;
      Frederick Bracker; Black Nevius; Claude-
      Edmonde Magny
4.   The Grapes of Wrath; Articles by M. S.
      Shockley; F. I. Carpenter; J. W. Beach
5.   The Later Work: Articles by Antonia Sexas
      (tj.); Peter Lisca; J. W. Krutch
      A Postscript from Steinbeck: 2 articles
      A Checklist of Steinbeck's Books
      See II, B, 3.

Watt, Frank William. John Steinbeck. London: Oliver
and Boyd, 1962.
(Writers and Critics Series, Ed. by A. Norman
Jeffares.)
Also Evergreen Pilot EP 13. New York: Grove
Press, 1962.

Contents:
1.   Steinbeck and His Sea of Cortez
2.   The Long Valley
3.   The Angry Thirties
4.   The Later Steinbeck
5.   A Note on the Critics

Bibliography
See II, B, 3.

Wilson, James Robert. "Responses of College
Freshmen To Three Novels. " Unpublished Ed. D.
dissertation, University of California, 1963.
J. D. Salinger, The Catcher in the Rye; John
Steinbeck, The Grapes of Wrath; and Ernest Heming-
way, A Farewell to Arms.

Young, Leo Vernon. "Values of the Young Characters
in the Fiction of Dos Passos, Hemingway, and
Steinbeck. " Unpublished Ph.d. dissertation, Stanford University, 1957.
Also in Dissertation Abstracts, XVIII (1958), 518-
519.

2. Discussion of Steinbeck's Works in Books

Adams, James Donald. "John Steinbeck - Main Street
and The Dust Bowl, " in The Shape of Books to
Come. New York: Viking Press, 1948. pp. 136-140.

Allen, Walter. Tradition & Dream: The English &
American Novel From the Twenties to Our Time.
London: Phoenix House, 1963. (Reprinted as The
Modern Novel in Britain & The United States. N. Y. :
Dutton, 1964) pp. 161-166 in both editions.

Allen Walter. The Modern Novel in Britain & The
United States, N. Y. : Dutton, 1964. pp. 161-166.
See also his Tradition & Dream.

Angoff, Allan (ed.). "John Steinbeck, " in American
Writing Today: Its Independence and Vigor. New
York: New York University Press, 1957. Passim.

Armitage, Merle. "John Steinbeck, " in Accent on
America. New York: E. Weyhe, 1944. pp. 271-272.

Beach, Joseph Warren. "Art & Propaganda, " in
American Fiction, 1920-40. N. Y. : Russell &
Russell, 1960. Scholars' Classics RP7. pp. 325-347.

Beach, Joseph Warren. "John Steinbeck: Art and
Propaganda, " in American Fiction, 1920-1940.
New York: Macmillan, 1941.

Also in Tedlock, Ernest W. , Jr. and Wicker, C. V.
(eds.) Steinbeck and His Critics. pp. 250-265.

Beach, Joseph Warren. "John Steinbeck: Journeyman
Artist, " in American Fiction, 1920-1940. New York:
Macmillan, 1941. pp. 309-347.
Also in Tedlock, Ernest W. , Jr. , and Wicker, C. V.
(eds.) Steinbeck and His Critics.
See II, A.

Blair, Walter, et al. (eds.). "John Steinbeck, " in The
Literature of the United States. 3 vols. Chicago:
Scott, Foresman & Co. , 1953. Passim.
See II, A.

Blankenship, Russell. "John Steinbeck and The
Sociological Novel, " in American Literature as an
Expression of the National Mind. New York: Holt,
Rinehart & Winston, 1958. pp. 745-749.

Block, Maxine (ed.) "John Steinbeck" Current Biography.
New York: Wilson, 1940. pp. 757-759.

Blotner, Joseph L. "John Steinbeck: The Party
Organizer, " in The Political Novel. Garden City,
N. Y. : Doubleday, 1955. p. 14.
See II, A.

Boynton, Percy Holmes. "John Steinbeck, " in America
in Contemporary Fiction. Chicago: University of
Chicago Press, 1940. pp. 241-257.

Bracher, Frederick. "Steinbeck and the Biological
View of Man, " The Pacific Spectator, II (Winter,
1948), 14-29.
Also in Steinbeck and His Critics. Edited by Ernest
W. Tedlock, Jr. & C. V. Wicker. pp. 183-196.

Bradley, Sculley, et al. (eds.). "John Steinbeck, " in
The American Tradition in Literature. V. II.
New York: W. W. Norton , 1962. pp. 1399-1401.

Braley, Berton. "Acknowledgment (to John Steinbeck),"
in Morgan Sails the Caribbean. New York:
Macmillan, 1934, pp. vii-viii.
The author explains his indebtness to Steinbeck's
Cup of Gold.

See I. K.

Brewster, Dorothy and Burrell, John A. "John Steinbeck: Artist with a Message," in Modern World of Fiction. New Jersey: Littlefield & Adams & Co., 1953.

Brown, Deming. "John Steinbeck," in Soviet Attitudes Toward American Writing. Princeton, N.J.: Princeton University Press, 1962. Passim.

Brown, Deming. "Soviet Criticism of American Proletarian Literature of the 1930's," in American Contributions to the Fourth International Congress of Slavicists, Moscow, September, 1958. The Hague: Mouton, 1958. p. 2.

Brown, John Mason. "Mr. Steinbeck's Of Mice and Men," in Two on the Aisle; Ten Years of the American Theatre in Performance. New York: W. W. Norton, 1938. pp. 183-187.
See II, B, 3.

Burgum, Edwin Berry. "Fickle Sensibility of John Steinbeck," in The Novel and the World's Dilemma. New York: Oxford University Press, 1947. pp. 272-291.
Also in SHC, pp. 104-118.

Burgum, Edwin Berry. "The Sensibility of John Steinbeck," Science and Society, X (Spring, 1946), 132-147.
Also in Steinbeck and His Critics. Edited by Ernest W. Tedlock, Jr., & C. V. Wicker. pp. 104-118.

Burke, Kenneth. The Philosophy of Literary Form. Baton Rouge: Louisiana State University Press, 1941. Passim.

Coan, Otis W. & Richard G. Lillard. America in Fiction. Palo Alto, California: Stanford University, 1949. pp. 64, 73, 132, 171.

Commager, Henry Steele. The American Mind. New Haven: Yale University Press, 1950. pp. 271-273.

Cournas, John, and Sybil Norton. Famous Modern American Novelists. New York: Dodd, Mead, 1952. pp. 153-157.

Covici, Pascal (ed.). "Introduction," in The Portable Steinbeck. New York: Viking Press, 1946. pp. vii-xxx.

Cowley, Malcolm. "Steinbeck," in The Literary Situation. New York: Viking, 1955. Passim.

Cunliffe, Marcus. "Fiction Since World War I." The Literature of the United States. London: Penguin, 1954. Passim.

Daiches, David. "Steinbeck" in A Study of Literature for Readers & Critics. Ithaca: Cornell University, 1948. pp. 63-64, 94, 132.

De Voto, Bernard. The World of Fiction. Boston: Houghton Mifflin Co., 1950. Passim.

Dickinson, Asa Don. "Steinbeck" in The Best Books of the Decade 1936-1945: Another Clue to the Literary Lobybrinter. New York: H. W. Wilson Co., 1948. pp. 208-210.

Dunaway, Philip, and Evans, Melvin (eds.). "John Steinbeck," in Treasury of the World's Great Diaries. Garden City, N. Y.: Doubleday, 1957. pp. 316-323.

The Editors of Fortune. "I Wonder Where We Can Go Now," in French (ed.), A Companion to The Grapes of Wrath. pp. 31-42.

Eisinger, Chester E. "Steinbeck," in Fiction of the Forties. Chicago & London: The University of Chicago Press, 1964. pp. 4, 10, 48, 50-51, 100-101, 331, 333, 369.

Fiedler, Leslie A. "Steinbeck," in Waiting for the End. New York: Stein & Day Publishers, 1964. Passim.

Freiman, Ray. (ed.). "Some Random and Randy Thoughts
in Books" in The Author Looks at Format, New
York: Trade Borre Clinic, 1950-51.

French, Warren G. "Steinbeck, " in Encyclopedia
Americana. Vol. 25 New York.: Americana Corp.,
1964. p. 612.
See II, A.

French, Warren G. "Steinbeck" in J. D. Salinger.
New York: Twayne Publishers, Inc., 1963. pp.
43, 84, 106. (The Grapes of Wrath, Cannery Row,
The Pastures of Heaven)
See II, B, 3.

French, Warren. "John Steinbeck" in his The Social
Novel at the End of an Era. Southern Illinois
University Press, 1966. pp. 42-86; 157-170.

Friede, Donald. The Mechanical Angel. New York:
Knopf, 1948. pp. 126-132. Et Passim.

Frohock, William M. "John Steinbeck --- The Utility
of Wrath, " in The Novel of Violence in America.
Dallas, Texas: Southern Methodist University Press,
1950. Passim.

Fuller, Edmund. "John Steinbeck, " in Man in Modern
Fiction: Some Minority Opinions on Contemporary
American Writing. New York: Random House, 1958.
Passim.

Gannett, Lewis. "Introduction, " in Portable Steinbeck.
Edited by Pascal Covici. New York: Viking Press,
1958. pp. vii-xviii.

Gannett, Lewis. "John Steinbeck, " in Preface to The
Cup of Gold. New York: Collier, 1936. pp. v-viii.
See II, B, 3.

Gannett, Lewis. "John Steinbeck's Way of Writing, "
in Steinbeck and His Critics. Edited by Ernest W.
Tedlock, Jr. & C. V. Wicker. Albuquerque: University of New Mexico Press, 1957. pp. 23-37.

Gardiner, Harold Charles. "Novelist To Philosopher?"
in In All Conscience: Reflections on Books & Culture.

Garden City, N. Y.: Hanover House, 1959. pp. 136-138. (East of Eden.)
See II, B, 3.

Geismar, Maxwell David. "Further Decline of the Moderns: John Steinbeck," in American Moderns, From Rebellion to Conformity. New York: Hill & Wang, 1958. pp. 151-156, 164-167. Passim.

Geismar, Maxwell David. "John Steinbeck: Of Wrath or Joy," in Writers in Crisis: The American Novels, 1925-1940. Boston: Houghton Mifflin, 1942. pp. 237-270.
See II, B, 3.

Gerould, Gordon Hall. "Steinbeck," in The Patterns of English and American Fiction. Boston: D. C. Heath & Co., 1942. pp. 490-491.

Gibbs, Lincoln R. "J. S., Moralist," in SHC, pp. 92-103.
Also in Antioch Review, II (June, 1942), 172-184.

Gide, Andre. The Journals of Andre Gide. Translated by Justin O'Brien. New York: Knopf, 1947.
(September 27, 1940; July 29, 1941)

Gray, James. "A Local Habitation in John Steinbeck," in On Second Thought. Minneapolis: University of Minnesota Press, 1946. pp. 133-140.

Gray, James. "Steinbeck," in On Second Thought. Minneapolis: University of Minnesota, 1946. pp. 133-140.

Gurko, Leo. "Steinbeck," Heroes, Highbrows and the Popular Mind. New York: Bobbs-Merrill Co., 1953. Passim.

Haines, Helen E. "Steinbeck," What's In a Novel. New York: Ronald Press Co., 1935. Passim.

Hart, James D. "Steinbeck," The Popular Book. New York: Oxford University Press, 1950. pp. 250, 272.

Hart, James D. (ed.). "Steinbeck," in The Oxford

Companion To American Literature. New York:
Oxford University Press, 1956. pp. 722-723.

Hastings, William T. "John Steinbeck," in Syllabus of
American Literature. Chicago: University of Chicago
Press, 1941. pp. 103; 105-106.

Hedley, George. "Steinbeck," in Background and Fore-
grounds. Mills College, Oakland: The Eucalyptus
Press, 1939. Passim.

Heiney, Donald. "American Naturalism & the New
Italian Writers," Twentieth Century Literature, III
(October, 1957), p. 135-141.

Heiney, Donald W. "Steinbeck," in Essentials of
Contemporary Literature. Great Neck, N.Y.:
Barron's, Educational Series, 1954. pp. 143-146.

Henderson, Caroline A. "Letters from the Dust Bowl,"
in French (ed.), A Companion to The Grapes of
Wrath. pp. 15-27.

Herzberg, Max J. and The Staff of The Thomas Y.
Crowell Co. (eds.). "John Ernst Steinbeck," in
The Reader's Encyclopedia of American Literature.
New York: Crowell, 1962. pp. 1079-1080.
See II, A.

Hicks, Granville (ed.). "Steinbeck," Proletarian
Literature in the United States. New York:
International Publishers, 1935. Passim.

Hinkel, Edgar J. and McCann, William E. Criticism
of California Literature. Oakland, California:
Alaweda County Library, 1940. Official Project No.
665-08-3-85 of Work Project. Administration.
Mimeographed.

Hoffman, Frederick J. "Steinbeck," in The Modern
Novel in America 1900-1950. Chicago: Henry Regney
Co., 1951. pp. 137, 146-153, 185.

Hoffman, Frederick J. "Violence & Rhetoric in the
1930's," The Modern Novel in America. Chicago:
Regney, 1951. 160-168.

Howard, Leon. "Power & The Past: John Steinbeck," in Literature and the American Tradition. Garden City, N. Y.: Doubleday, 1960. pp. 301-303.

Howard, Leon. "Steinbeck," in Literature & The American Tradition. Garden City, N. Y.: Doubleday & Co., Inc., 1960. pp. 301-303.

Hyman, Stanley E. "Some Notes on John Steinbeck," in SHC., pp. 152-166.
Also in Antioch Review, II (June, 1942), pp. 185-200.

Hyman, Stanley Edgar. "John Steinbeck, Of Invertebrates & Men" in this The Promised End. Cleveland World Publishing Co., 1963. pp. 17-22.

Jackson, Joseph Henry. "The Finest Book John Steinbeck Has Written," in French (ed.), A Companion to The Grapes of Wrath. pp. 111-117.

Jackson, Joseph Henry. "Steinbeck," in "Introduction," to The Grapes of Wrath. New York: Limited Edition Club and Heritage Press, 1940.
See II, B, 3.

Jackson, Joseph Henry. "Steinbeck," in "Introduction," To Of Mice and Men. New York: Random House, Modern Library, 1937.
See II, B, 3.

Jackson, Joseph Henry. "John Steinbeck," in the Preface to The Short Novels of John Steinbeck. New York: Viking Press, 1963. pp. vii-xv.
See II, B, 2.

Karsh, Yousuf. "Steinbeck," Portraits of Greatness. New York: Nelson, 1959.

Kazin, Alfred. "John Steinbeck," in On Native Grounds: An Interpretation of Modern American Prose Literature. New York: Reynal & Hitchcock, 1942. pp. 393-399.

Kazin, Alfred. "The Revival of Naturalism," On Native Grounds, pp. 393-399.

Kennedy, John S. "John Steinbeck: Life Affirmed and

Dissolved, " in Steinbeck and His Critics. Edited by
Ernst W. Tedlock, Jr. , and C. V. Wicker. Albuquerque: University of New Mexico Press, 1957.
pp. 119-134.
Also in Gardiner, Harold C. (ed.). Fifty Years of
the American Novel. New York: Scribner's, 1951.
pp. 217-236.

Kennedy, John S. "John Steinbeck: Life Affirmed and
Dissolved," in Steinbeck and His Critics. Edited by
Ernest W. Tedlock, Jr. & C. V. Wicker. Albu-
querque: University of New Mexico Press, 1957.
pp. 119-134.
Also in Fifty Years of the American Novel, Harold
C. Gardiner. New York: Scribner's, 1951. pp. 217-
236.

Kroneberger, Louis. "Hungry Caravan, " College Prose.
Edited by Theodore Gates & Austin Wright. Boston:
D. C. Heath, 1942. pp. 424-427.

Krutch, Joseph Wood, "Steinbeck, " in The American
Drama Since 1918: An Informal History. New York:
Random House, 1939. pp. 128-130, 139. (Of Mice
& Men; The Grapes of Wrath)

Kunitz, Stanley J. (ed.). "John Steinbeck, " in Twentieth
Century Authors; A Biographical Dictionary of
Modern Literature. 1st Supplement. New York:
H. W. Wilson, 1955. pp. 954-955.

Leighton, M. M. "Geology of Soil Drifting on the Great
Plains, " in French (ed.), A Companion to The Grapes
of Wrath. pp. 8-15.

Lewis, R. W. B. "The Steinbeck Perspective, " in The
Picaresque Saint; Representative Figures in Contemporary Fiction. Philadelphia: Lippincott, 1958.
pp. 179-193.

Lewis, R. W. B. "John Steinbeck: The Fitful Daemon,"
in The Young Rebel in American Literature. Edited
by Carl Bode. New York: Frederick A. Praeger,
1960. pp. 121-141.
Also in Modern American Fiction: Essays in
Criticism. Edited by A. Walton Litz. New York:
Oxford University Press, 1963. pp. 265-277.

Lisca, Peter. "John Ernst Steinbeck," Collier's
Encyclopedia, 1964. XXI, p. 518.

Lisca, Peter. "John Ernst Steinbeck," Encyclopedia
Britannica, 1964. XXI, p. 377.

Lisca, Peter. "John Steinbeck: A Literary Biography,"
in Steinbeck and His Critics. Edited by Ernst W.
Tedlock, Jr. & C. V. Wicker, Albuquerque:
University of New Mexico Press, 1957. pp. 3-22.

Lisca, Peter. "Steinbeck's Fable of the Pearl," in
Steinbeck and His Critics. Edited by Ernst W.
Tedlock, Jr. & C. V. Wicker. Albuquerque:
University of New Mexico Press, 1957. pp. 291-301.
First appeared in his Ph. D. dissertation, "The Art
of John Steinbeck," 1955.

Lisca, Peter. "The Wayward Bus - a Modern Pilgrimage," in Steinbeck and His Critics. Edited by
Ernest W. Tedlock, Jr. & C. V. Wicker. Albuquerque: University of New Mexico Press, 1957.
pp. 281-290.
First appeared in his Ph. D. dissertation, "The Art
of John Steinbeck," 1955.
See II, B, 3.

Luccock, Halford E. "Of Mortgages and Migrants," in
American Mirror: Social, Ethical and Religious
Aspects of American Literature, 1930-1940. pp. 179-
185.

Luccock, Halford E. "Steinbeck," in American Mirror:
Social, Ethical and Religious Aspects of American
Literature, 1930-1940. New York: The Macmillan
Co., 1940. pp. 179-185. Passim.

McWilliams, Carey. "The End of a Cycle," in French
(ed.), A Companion to The Grapes of Wrath, pp.
42-49.

McWilliams, Carey. "Glory, Glory, California," in
French (ed.), A Companion to The Grapes of Wrath.
pp. 140-143.

Magill, Frank N. (ed.). "John Steinbeck," in Cyclopedia
of World Authors. New York: Salem Press, 1958.

pp. 1017-1019.

Magney, Claude-Edmonde. "Steinbeck, or the Limits
of the Impersonal Novel," in Steinbeck and His
Critics. Edited by Ernest W. Tedlock, Jr., & C. V.
Wicker. Albuquerque: University of New Mexico
Press, 1957. pp. 216-230.
First appeared in his L'Age du Roman Americain.
Translated by Francoise Gourier.

Mallett, Richard. "The Steinbeck Party," in Twentieth
Century Parody, Edited by Burling Lowrey. Intro-
duced by N. Benchley. New York: Harcourt, Brace
& Co., 1960. p. 81.

Marchwardt, Albert H. "Regional and Social Variations,"
in Introductory Readings on Language. Edited by
Wallace L. Anderson and Norman C. Stageberg.
New York: Holt, Rinehart & Winston, Inc., 1962.
pp. 327-328. (Steinbeck & His Use of Dialects)

Mendelson, M. "Steinbeck," in Soviet Interpretation of
Contemporary American Literature. Washington,
D. C.: Public Affairs Press, 1948. Passim.

Millett, Fred B. "John Steinbeck," in Contemporary
American Authors: A Critical Survey & 219 Bio-
Bibliographies. New York: Harcourt, Brace & Co.,
1944. pp. 50; 596-597.
See III.

Mizener, Arthur. The Sense of Life in the Modern
Novel. Boston: Houghton Mifflin, 1964. pp. 6, 20,
128.

Moritz, Charles (ed.). "Steinbeck," in Current
Biography. New York: H. W. Wilson, 1940. pp.
757-759.
See III

Morris, Lloyd R. "Seven Pillars of Wisdom," in
Postscript to Yesterday; America: Last Fifty Years.
New York: Random House, 1947. pp. 134-171.

Moskovic, Armin (tr.).
See Orlova, R.

Mott, Frank L. "Steinbeck, " Golden Multitude, New York: Macmillan, 1947. p. 259, Et Passim.

Nevins, Blake. "Steinbeck: One Aspect, " SHC, pp. 197-206.

Nyren, Dorothy (ed.). "Steinbeck, " in A Library of Literary Criticism: Modern American Literature. New York: Frederick Ungar Publishing Company, 1960. pp. 465-468.
    P. 466: Edmund C. Richards, NAR, (June, 1937), p. 409.
        Burton Rascoe, EJ (March, 1938), pp. 213-4.
        T. K. Whipple, NR (October 12, 1938), p. 294.
    P. 466: Edmund Wilson, NR (December 9, 1940), pp. 785-786.
        Maxwell Geisman, Writers in Crisis (Houghton), 1942. p. 260.
        Woodburn O. Ross, CE (May, 1949), pp. 436-437.
    p. 467: Blake Nevins, PS (Summer, 1949), pp. 307-308.
        W. M. Brohock, The Novel of Violence in America. (S M University Press, 1940), p. 147.
        Joseph Henry Jackson, Introduction to The Short Novels of John Steinbeck. (Viking, 1953), pp. vii-viii.
        Hugh Holman, NR (June 7, 1954), p. 20.
        Claude-Edmonde Mogny in Steinbeck and His Critics, ed. by F. W. Tedlock & C. V. Wilken (N. Y. N. M. Press, 1957), pp. 225-227.

O'Brien, Justin (translation). See Gide, Andre.

O'Hara, F. H. "Melodrama With a Meaning, " in Today in American Drama. Chicago: University of Chicago Press, 1939. pp. 142-189.

Orlova, R. "Money Against Humanity: Notes on the Work of John Steinbeck, " translation by Armin Moskovic. In French (ed.), A Companion to The Grapes of Wrath, pp. 152-159.

Powell, Lawrence Clark. "Steinbeck" in Books in My Baggage. Cleveland & New York: World Publishing

Co., 1960. pp. 87, 175, 208, 238.

Powell, Lawrence Clark. "Steinbeck," in Southwestern
Book Trails. A Reader's Guide to the Heartland of
New Mexico & Arizona. Albuquerque: Horn &
Wallace, Publishers, 1963. p. 31.

Prescott, Orville. "Squandered Talents: Lewis, Steinbeck, Hemingway, O'Hara," in In My Opinion.
Indianapolis: Bobbs-Merrill, 1952. pp. 50-74.

Priestley, J. B. "Steinbeck" in Literature & Western
Man. New York: Harper & Brothers, 1960. p. 433.
(The Grapes of Wrath)

Quinn, Arthur Hobson, et al, "Steinbeck," in The
Literature of the American People. New York:
Appleton-Century-Crofts, 1951. pp. 958-961.

Rascoe, Burton. "John Steinbeck," SHC, pp. 57-67.

Raymund, Bernard. "John Steinbeck," in his Writers
of Today. London: Sidgwick, 1946. pp. 122-138.

Reynolds, Quentin. "Steinbeck," The Curtain Rises.
New York: Random House, 1944. Passim.

Rexroth, Kenneth. Afterword to Frank Norris, Mc-
TEAGUE. New York: New American Library, 1964
(Signet). Contains Reference to John Steinbeck in
Connection with "The Boys in the Back Room" by
Edmund Wilson.
See also Wilson, Edmund.

Rideout, Walter S. "Steinbeck," The Radical Novel in
the United States 1900-1954. Cambridge, Mass.:
Harvard University Press, 1956. Passim.

Rosenblatt, Louise M. "Steinbeck," in Literature as
Exploration. New York: D. Appleton-Century Co.,
1938. Passim.

Ross, Woodburn O. "John Steinbeck: Earth and Stars,"
in Steinbeck and His Critics. Edited by Ernest W.
Tedlock, Jr. & C. V. Wicker. Albuquerque: University of New Mexico Press, 1957. pp. 167-182.
First appeared in The University of Missouri Studies

in Honor of A. H. R. Fairchild, XXI. Columbia: University of Missouri Press, 1946. pp. 179-197.

Ross, Woodburn O. "John Steinbeck, Naturalism's Priest," SHC, pp. 206-215.
Also in College English, X (May, 1949), pp. 432-438.

Rubin, Louis D. & Moore, John Rees (editors). "Steinbeck," in The Idea of an American Novel. New York: Thomas Y. Crowell Co., 1961. pp. 172-173.

Scherman, David Edward and Rosemarie Redliche. "Steinbeck," Literary America. New York: n. d., pp. 166-167.

Schorer, Mark. "Technique as Discovery," in Forms of Modern Fiction. Edited by W. Van O'Connor. Bloomington: Indiana University Press, 1959. pp. 9-29.

Scully, Frank. "Steinbeck," in Rogues' Gallery: Profiles of My Eminent Contemporaries. Hollywood: Murray & Gee, 1943. pp. 37-55.

Seixas, Antonia (Toni Ricketts). "John Steinbeck and the Non-Teleological Bus," in Steinbeck and His Critics. Edited by Ernest W. Tedlock, Jr. & C. V. Wicker. Albuquerque: University of New Mexico Press, 1957. pp. 275-280.

Shannon, David A. (editor). The Great Depression. Englewood Cliffs, N. J.: Prentice, 1960.

Slochower, Harry. "John Dos Passos & John Steinbeck, Contrasting Notions of the Communal Personality," in Byrdcliffe Afternoons. Edited by C. E. Jones. Woodstock, N. Y.: Overlook Press, 1940. pp. 11, 21.

Slochower, Harry. "The Promise of America," in his No Voice is Wholly Lost. New York: Creative Age Press, 1945. pp. 299-308.
Also in his Literature and Philosophy Between Two World Wars: The Problem in a War Culture. New York: Citadel Press, 1964. pp. 299-306.

Slochower, Harry. "Towards a Communal Personality,"

in No Voice is Wholly Lost. New York: Creative Age Press, 1945. pp. 242-248.

Smith, Thelma M., and Miner, Ward L. "John Steinbeck," in Transatlantic Migration: The Contemporary American Novel in France. Durham: Duke University Press, 1955. pp. 24-25; 161-178.

Snell, George D. "John Steinbeck: Realistic Whimsy," in The Shape of American Fiction 1798-1947. New York: Dutton, 1947. pp. 187-197.

Spiller, Robert E. "John Steinbeck," in The Cycle of American Literature: An Essay in Historical Criticism. New York: New American Library, 1956. Passim.

Spiller, Robert E., et al. (eds.). "John Steinbeck," in Literary History of the United States: History. 4 vols. New York: Macmillan, 1963. Passim.

"Steinbeck," Always Something to Do in Salinas: The World of Mankind, Edited by Ted Patrick. New York: The Golden Press, (n.c.). p. 318. (Selected by the Writers, Photographers & Editors of Holiday.)

Stern, Milton R. & Seymour R. Gross (eds.). "Steinbeck," in Am. Lit. Survey. IV. Twentieth Century. New York: Viking Portable Library, 1962. pp. 171-174.

Stovall, Floyd. "Contemporary Fiction," in American Idealism. Norman: University of Oklahoma Press, 1943. pp. 159-166.

Straumann, Heinrich. "Steinbeck," in American Literature in the Twentieth Century. New York: Hutchinson's University Library, 1951.
(Also by Watford, Hertsfordshire: The Mayflower Press, 1951), pp. 107-111. The Moon is Down.

Struve, Gleb. "Steinbeck," Soviet Russian Literature. Norman: University of Oklahoma Press, 1951. Passim

Tannehill, Ivan Ray. "Dusters and Black Blizzards," in Warren French (ed.), A Companion to The Grapes of Wrath. New York: Viking, 1964. pp. 5-81.

Taylor, Walter Fuller. "John Steinbeck," in The Story
of American Letters. Chicago: Henry Regnery, 1956.
pp. 457-460.

Thorp, Willard. "Steinbeck," American Writing in the
Twentieth Century. Cambridge, Mass.: Harvard
University Press, 1960. pp. 130-132.

Trilling, Lionel. "Steinbeck," in The Liberal Imagination. New York: Viking Press, 1950. Passim.

Uzzell, Thomas H. "The Grapes of Wrath" in The
Technique of the Novel. New York: Citadel Press,
1964. pp. 231 & Passim.
See II, B, 3.

Van Doren, Carl Clinton. "Steinbeck," in "Introduction,"
to The Grapes of Wrath. Cleveland: World Publishing Co., 1947.
See II, B, 3.

Van Doren, Carl Clinton (ed.). "Revisions," in
American Novel, 1789-1939. New York: Macmillan,
1960. pp. 349-366.

Van Doren, M. "Wrong Number," in Private Reader.
New York: Holt, 1942. pp. 255-257.

Wagenknecht, Edward Charles. "Two Kinds of
Novelist: Steinbeck & Marquand," in Cavalcade of
the American Novel, From the Birth of the Nation
to the Middle of the Twentieth Century. New York:
Holt, 1952. pp. 438-448.

Walcutt, Charles Child. "Later Trends in Form:
Steinbeck, Hemingway, Dos Passos," in American
Literary Naturalism, A Divided Stream. Minneapolis:
University of Minnesota Press, 1956. pp. 258-265;
267-270.

Warfel, Harry Redcay. "John Steinbeck," in American
Novelists of Today. New York: American Book Co.,
1951. pp. 403-405.

Whicher, George F. "Proletarian Leanings," in The
Literature of the American People. Edited by Arthur
Hobson Quinn. New York: Appleton-Century Crofts,

1951. pp. 958-961. (The Grapes of Wrath).

Whipple, Thomas King. "Steinbeck: Through a Glass Though Brightly," in Study Out the Land. Berkeley & Los Angeles: University of California Press, 1945. pp. 105-111.

Williams, Stanley T. "John Steinbeck," in The Spanish Background of American Literature. New Haven, Conn.: Yale University Press, 1955. I, Passim.

Wilson, Edmund. "The Boys in the Back Room," Classics & Commercials. New York: Farrar, Straus & Young, 1950. pp. 34-45.
See also Rexroth, Kenneth.

Wilson, Edmund. "John Steinbeck," in The Boys in the Back Room. San Francisco: Colt Press, 1941. pp. 41-53.
Also in his Classics and Commercials. New York: Farrar, Straus, 1950, pp. 35-45.

Wilson, Edmund. "Steinbeck," Classics & Commercials, A Literary Chronicle of the Forties. New York: Farrar, Straus, 1950. Passim.

Wilson, Edmund. "John Steinbeck," in Boys in the Back Room; Notes on California Novelists. San Francisco: Colt Press, 1941. pp. 41-53.
Also as "The Boys in the Back Room," in Classics and Commercials. New York: Farrar, Straus, 1950. pp. 35-45.

Winter, Ella. And Not to Yield, An Autobiography. New York: Harcourt, Brace & World, 1963. "Steinbeck," pp. 129, 212-213, 240.

Witham, W. Tasker. "John Steinbeck," in Panorama of American Literature. New York: Ungar, 1947. pp. 340-345.

3. Book Reviews and Critical Essays

Abramson, Ben. "John Steinbeck," in Reading and Collecting, I (December, 1936), 4-5; 18.
See II, A.

"Assisting John Steinbeck, " Newsweek, XLVII (June, 1956), 56.
See II, A.

"Authors and Others, " Publisher's Weekly, CXXVIII (July 27, 1935), 223.
See II, A.

Baker, Carlos. "Forty Years of Pulitzer Prizes. " Princeton University Library Chronicle, XVIII (Winter, 1957), 55-70.

Baker, Carlos. "The Pulitzer Prizes, 1917-1957: Fiction Awards. " Columbia Literary Columns, VI (May, 1957), 30-34.

Baker, Carlos. "Steinbeck at the Top of His Form, " New York Times Book Review, November 30, 1947. pp. 4, 52.

Baker, Carlos. "Steinbeck of California, " Delphian Quarterly, XXIII (April, 1940), 40-45.

Baker, Howard. "In Praise of the Novel, " Southern Review, V, (1940), 778-800.

Beach, Joseph Warren. "Eight Novelists Between Wars, " Saturday Review of Literature XXIII (March 29, 1941), 3.

Berkelman, R. G. "George Sterling on 'The Black Vulture'. " American Literature, X (May, 1938), 223-224.

"Bernie Byrens Files Breach of Contract Suit Against John Steinbeck, L. Milestone, and B. Meredith, " New York Times, February 24, 1948. p. 22.
See II, A.

Bidwell, Martin. "John Steinbeck: An Impression, " Prairie Schooner, XII (Spring, 1938), 10-15.
See II, A.

Blanck, Jacob (ed.). "American First Editions, " Publishers' Weekly, CXXXI (April 17, 1937), 1701. John Steinbeck Checklist by Lawrence C. Powell.
See III.

Bracher, Frederic. "California's Literary Regionalism,"
American Quarterly, VII (Fall, 1955), 275-285.

Bregy, Katherine. "Of John Steinbeck, " America, LXXI
(August 19, 1944), 496-497.
See II, A.

Brown, Daniel R. "A Monolith of Logic Against Waves
of Nonsense, " Renascence, XVI (Fall, 1963),
48-51.

Brustein, Robert. "America's New Culture Hero:
Feelings Without Words, " Commentary, XXV
(February, 1958), 123-129.

Calder-Marshall, A. "Novels of John Steinbeck, "
Fortnightly, CLII (September, 1939), 295-304.

Calverton, V. F. "John Steinbeck: Fulfilment Without
Promise, " Modern Monthly, X (June, 1938),
11-12, 16.

Calverton, V. F. "Steinbeck, Hemingway, and
Faulkner, " Modern Quarterly, XI (Fall, 1939),
36-44.

Carpenter, Frederick I. "John Steinbeck: American
Dreamer, " The Southwest Review, XXVI (July, 1941),
454-467.
Also in Steinbeck and His Critics. Edited by Ernest
W. Tedlock, Jr. & C. V. Wicker. pp. 68-79.

Champney, Freeman. "Critics in Search of an Author, "
Antioch Review, XVIII (Fall, 1958), 371-375.

Champney Freeman. "John Steinbeck, Californian, "
Antioch Review, VII (September, 1947), 345-362.
Also in Steinbeck and His Critics. Edited by Ernest
W. Tedlock, Jr. & C. V. Wicker. pp. 135-151.
See II, A.

Chapin, Chester F. "Pepé Torres: A Steinbeck
'Natural', " College English, XXIII (May, 1962),
676.   "The Flight. "

Chase, Richard. "Radicalism in the American Novel, "
Commentary, XXIII (January, 1947), 65-71.

Chessex, J. C. "Fernand Gregh Chez John Steinbeck,"
Comparative Literature, X (Summer, 1958),
254-260.

Cody, W. F. "John Steinbeck Will Get You If You
Don't Watch Out, " Saturday Review of Literature,
XXVIII (July 7, 1945), 18-19.

Connolly, Francis X. "John Steinbeck, Prix Nobel, "
Transatlantic Review, CLXXX (January, 1963),
93-99.

Cousins, Norman. "Bankrupt Realism, " Saturday Review
of Literature, XXX (March 8, 1947), 22-23.

Cousins, Norman. "Hemingway & Steinbeck, " Saturday
Review of Literature, XXXIII (October 28, 1950),
26-27.

Cousins, Norman. "Who Are the Real People?"
Saturday Review of Literature, XXVIII (March 17,
1945), 14.

Cowley, Malcolm. "Sherwood Andersen's Epiphanies, "
London Magazine, VII (July, 1960), 61-66.

"Cutting Down the Laurels; Nobel Prize for Literature, "
New Republic, CXLVII (November 10, 1962), 8.

Davis, Elmer. "The Steinbeck Country, " Saturday
Review of Literature, XVIII (September 24, 1938),
11.

De Schweinitz, George. "Steinbeck & Christianity, "
College English, XIX (May, 1958), 369.

De Voto, Bernard. "American Novels: 1939, " Atlantic
Monthly, CLXV (January, 1940), 66-74.

"Death of a Racket, " Spectator, CXCIV (April 8, 1955),
430-431.

Dodds, John W. "The Mediocre American, " Huntington
Library Quarterly, XXII (May, 1959), 163-167.

Duhamel, P. Albert. "Love in the Modern Novel, "
Catholic World, CXCI (April, 1960), 31-35.

Dunn, T. F. "Bible and the Grapes of Wrath, " College English, XXIV (April, 1963), 566-567.
See H. K. Crockett's article on the same subject. (The Grapes of Wrath).

Eastman, Max. "John Steinbeck --- Genevieve Tabonis," The American Mercury, LIV (June, 1942), 754-756.

Fadiman, Clifton. "Steinbeck Again, " The New Yorker, XVIII (April 4, 1942), 55.

Fairley, Barker. "John Steinbeck and The Coming Literature, " Sewanee Review, C (April, 1942), 145-161.

Farrell, James T. "The End of a Literary Decade, " The American Mercury, XLVIII (December, 1939), 408-414.

Fazia, A. Della. "Nobel Prize, 1962 and the Bridge on the Drina Revisited, " Books Abroad, XXXVII (Winter, 1963), 24-26.

Fenton, Charles A. "The Writers Who Came Out of the War, " Saturday Review, XL (August 3, 1957), 5-7, 24.

Frey, John R. "Postwar German Reactions to American Literature, " Journal of English & German Philology, LIV (April, 1955), 173-194.

Frohock, William M. "John Steinbeck's Men of Wrath, " Southwest Review, XXXI (Spring, 1946), 144-152.

Fukuma, Ken-ichi. " 'Man' in Steinbeck's Works, " Kyushu American Literature, VII (1964), 21-30.

Gannett, Lewis. "John Steinbeck: Novelist at Work, " Atlantic Monthly, CLXXVI (December, 1945), 55-61.

Gannett, Lewis. "John Steinbeck: Novelist at Work, " Atlantic, CLXXVI (December, 1945), 55-60.

Geismar, Maxwell David. "Decline of the Classic Moderns, " Nation, CLXXX (May 7, 1955), 402-404.

Gerstenberger, Donna. "Steinbeck's American Waste
Land," Modern Fiction Studies, XI (Spring, 1965),
59-65.

Gibbs, Lincoln R. "John Steinbeck, Moralist," Antioch
Review, II (June, 1942), 172-184.
Also in Steinbeck and His Critics. pp. 92-103.
See II, A.

Gurko, Leo. "Steinbeck's Later Fiction," Nation,
CLXXV (September 20, 1952), 235-236.

Gurko, Leo, and Miriam. "The Steinbeck Temperament,"
Rocky Mountain Review, IX (Fall, 1954), 17-22.

"Have We Gone Soft?: America --- 1960, A Symposium,"
Thurston N. Davis; Arthur M. Schlesinger, Sr.;
Harry Golden; Reinhold Niebuhr. New Republic,
CXLII (February 15, 1960), 11-15.

Hester, Sister Mary. "Mr. Steinbeck? Frankly, No."
Today, XVII (May, 1963), 23-26.

Hicks, Granville. "The Thirties: A Reappraisal,"
Saturday Review, XLVI (May 4, 1963), 27-28.

Higashiyama, Masayoshi. "On Works of John Steinbeck, A Great Modern Novelist," Kansai Gakuin
Times, VII (1957), 15-28.

Hobson, L. Z. "Trade Winds," Saturday Review,
XXXV (August 30, 1952), 4.

Holman, C. Hugh. "A Narrow-gauge Dickens," New
Republic, CXXX (June 7, 1954), 18-20.   (Sweet
Thursday).

Hyman, Stanley E. "Some Notes on John Steinbeck,"
Antioch Review, II (June, 1942), 185-200.
Also in SHC, pp. 152-166.

Hyman, Stanley E. "Some Trends in the Novel,"
College English, XX (October, 1958), 1-9.

Inoue, Atsuko. "A Study of John Steinbeck: The Group
in His Fiction," Essays & Studies in British &
American Literature, Tokyo Women's Christian

College, XI (Winter, 1964), 49-99.

Isaacs, Edith J. R. "When Good Men Get Together," Theatre Arts Monthly, XXII (January, 1938), 13-16.

Isherwood, Christopher. "The Tragedy of El Dorado," Kenyon Review, I (Autumn, 1939), 450-453.

"John Steinbeck," Wilson Library Bulletin, XI (March, 1937), 456.
See II, A.

Johnson, Curtis L. "Steinbeck: A Suggestion for Research," MFS, XI (Spring, 1965), 75-78.

Jones, Claude Edward. "Proletarian Writing and John Steinbeck," Sewanee Review, XLVIII (October-December, 1940), 445-456.

Kalb, Bernard. "The Author," Saturday Review, XXXV (September 20, 1952), 11.
See II, A.

Kalb, Bernard. "Trade Winds," Saturday Review, XXXVI (February 27, 1954), 8.

Koike, Nobuo. "A Study of John Steinbeck With Special Reference to the Works in the 30's," British & American Literature, Kansei Gakuin University, III (April, 1954), 57-90.

Krutch, Joseph Wood. "John Steinbeck's Dramatic Tale of Three Generations," New York Herald Tribune Book Review, (September 21, 1952), p. 1.
Also in Steinbeck and His Critics. Edited by Ernest W. Tedlock, Jr., & C. V. Wicker. pp. 302-305.

Leonard, Frank G. "Cozzens Without Sex; Steinbeck Without Sin (Reader's Digest Condensed Books)," Antioch Review, XVIII (Summer, 1958), 209-218.

Levenson, Samuel. "Compassion of John Steinbeck," Canadian Forum, XX (September, 1940), 185-186.

Levidova, I. "The Post-War Books of John Steinbeck," Soviet Review, IV (Summer, 1963), 3-13.

Lisca, Peter. "A Letter on Criticism," Colorado Quarterly, IV (Autumn, 1955), 218-219.

Lisca, Peter. "Steinbeck's Image of Man & His Decline as a Writer," MFS, XI (Spring, 1965), 3-10.

McCormick, B. "John Steinbeck: An Evaluation," Way (U. S.), XIX (March, 1963), 53-58.

McHugh, V. "John Steinbeck Branches Out," American Mercury, XLVII (May, 1939), 113-115.

McKenney, J. W. "John Steinbeck Says a Great Teacher Is One of the Great Artists," California Teachers' Association Journal, LI (November, 1955), 6f.

McWilliams, Carey. "California Pastoral," Antioch Review, II (March, 1942), 103-121.

Marshall, Margaret. "Writers in the Wilderness," Nation, CXLIX (November 25, 1939), 576-579.

Mathiessen, F. O. "Some Philosophers in the Sun," New York Times, (December 31, 1944), 1, 18.

Marx, Leo. "Two Kingdoms of Force," Massachusetts Review, I (October, 1959), 62-95.

Mayo, Thomas F. "The Great Pendulum," Southwest Review, XXXVI (Summer, 1951), 190-201.

Mizener, Arthur. "Does a Moral Vision of the Thirties Deserve a Nobel Prize?" New York Times Book Review, December 9, 1962. pp. 4, 43-45.

Mizener, Arthur. "The Novel in America: 1920-1940," Perspectives USA, XV (Spring, 1956), 134-147.

Mizener, A. "In the Land of Nod," New Republic, CXXVII (October 6, 1952), 22-23.

Moloney, M. F. "Half-faith in Modern Fiction," Catholic World, CLXXI (August, 1950), 349-350.

Moore, Harry Thornton. "John Steinbeck the Soft-

Hearted Satirist, " New Republic, CXXXVI (May 27, 1959), 23-24.

Moore, Harry T. "Steinbeck the Soft-Hearted Artist, " New Republic, CXXXVI (May 27, 1957), 23-24.

Morioka, Sakae. "John Steinbeck's Art, " English & American Language & Literature Studies, Kyushu University, III (1953), 51-58.

Morris, Lloyd. "Heritage of a Generation of Novelists: Anderson & Dreiser, Hemingway, Faulkner, Farrell & Steinbeck, " New York Herald Tribune Weekly Book Review, XXV (September 25, 1949), pp. 12-13, 74.

Munro, Thomas. "The Failure Story: An Evaluation, " Journal of Aesthetics & Art Criticism, XVII (March, 1959), 362-387.

Munro, Thomas. "The Failure Story: A Study of Contemporary Pessimism, " Journal of Aesthetics & Art Criticism, XVII (December, 1958), 143-168.

Nebberger, Richard. "Who Are the Associated Farmers?" Survey Graphic, XXVIII (September, 1939), 517-521-555-557.

Nevius, Blake. "Steinbeck: One Aspect (His Attitude Toward Illusion), " The Pacific Spectator, III (Summer, 1949), 302-310.
Also in Steinbeck and His Critics. Edited by Ernest W. Tedlock, Jr. & C. V. Wicker. pp. 197-205.

North, Paul H. Jr. "Another Note on the Armed Services Edition (ASE), " American Book Collector, XV (November, 1964), 25.

Oliver, H. J. "John Steinbeck, " Australian Quarterly, XXIII (June, 1951), 79-83.

Peller, Lili E. "Daydreams and Children's Favorite Books, " The Psychoanalytic Study of the Child, XIV (1946), 414-433.

Powell, Lawrence Clark (ed.). "American First Editions, " Publishers' Weekly, CXXXI (April 17,

1937), 1701.
See III.

Powell, Lawrence Clark. "Toward a Bibliography of
John Steinbeck," The Colophon, III (Autumn, 1938),
558-568.
See III.

Prescott, Orville. "Outstanding Novels," Yale Review,
XXXVI (Autumn, 1947), 765.

Rascoe, Burton. "But ---- Not ---- Ferdinand,"
Newsweek, XIII (April 13, 1939), 46.

Rascoe, Burton. "Excuse It, Please," Newsweek,
XIII (May 1, 1939), 38.

Rascoe, Burton. "John Steinbeck," English Journal,
XXVII (March, 1938), 205-216.
Also in Steinbeck and His Critics. Edited by Ernest
W. Tedlock, Jr. & C. V. Wicker. pp. 57-67.

"Recording Writers," New York Times Magazine,
October 11, 1953. p. 44.

Redman, Ben Ray. "The Case of John Steinbeck,"
American Mercury, LXIV (May, 1947), 624-630.

Redman, Ben R. "French Romance," Saturday Review,
XL (April 13, 1957), 14.   On The Short Reign of
Pippin IV.

Richards, Edmund C. "The Challenge of John Steinbeck," North American Review, CCXLIII (June,
1937), 406-413.

Ross, Woodburn O. "John Steinbeck: Naturalism's
Priest," College English, X (May, 1949), 432-
438.
Also in Steinbeck and His Critics. Edited by Ernest
W. Tedlock, Jr. & C. V. Wicker. pp. 206-215.

Rundell, Walter, Jr. "Steinbeck's Image of the West,"
The American West, I (Spring, 1964), 4-17, 79.

Sanford, Charles L. "Classics of American Reform
Literature," American Quarterly, X (Fall, 1958),

295-311.

Sartre, Jean-Paul. "American Novelists in French
Eyes," Atlantic, CLXXVIII (August, 1946), 114-
118.
See II, 1, A.

Schramm, Wilber L. "Careers at Cross Roads,"
Virginia Quarterly Review, XV (October, 1939),
628-632.

Slochower, Harry. "The Promise of America," in No
Voice is Wholly Lost. New York: Creative Age
Press, 1945. pp. 299-308.
Also in his Literature and Philosophy Between Two
World Wars: The Problem in a War Culture. New
York: Citadel Press, 1964. pp. 299-306.
See II, B, 2.

Smith, H. "Is John Steinbeck Literary?" Teacher's
College Journal, XIII (January, 1942), 61-63.

Smith, James Stell. "Life Looks at Literature,"
American Scholar, XXVII (Winter, 1952-58), 24-
42.

Stevens, G. "Steinbeck's Uncovered Wagons," Saturday
Review of Literature, XIX (April 15, 1939), 3-4.

Strauss, Harold. "Realism in the Proletarian Novel,"
Yale Review, XXVIII (Winter, 1939), 360-374.

The Swedish Academy & The Nobel Prizes: Its Official
Statement is Quoted: Contemporary Authors, VII.
Michigan Yale Research Co., 1963. p. 184.
See II, A.

Tanner, Henry. "Steinbeck and Albee Speak Out in
Soviet for U. S. Professor," New York Times,
November 15, 1963. pp. 1, 5.

Tarr, E. Whitney. "Steinbeck on One Plane," Letter
to the Editor, Saturday Review of Literature, XXX
(December 20, 1947), 20.

Taylor, Horace Platt, Jr., "The Biological Naturalism
of John Steinbeck," McNeese Review, XII (Winter,

1960-61), 81-97.

Tuttleton, James W. "Steinberg in Russia: The Rhetoric of Praise & Blame, " MFS, XI (Spring, 1965), 79-89.

Van Gelder, Robert. "Interview with a Best-Selling Author: John Steinbeck, " Cosmopolitan, CXXII (April, 1947), 18. 123+. Reprint from Writers & Writing. New York: Scribners, 1946. See II, A.

Warren, Robert Penn. "A Fine Anthology of Steinbeck's Writings, " New York Times Book Review, August 22, 1943. p. 6. Review: The Portable Steinbeck.

Webster, Harvey C. "Out of the New-Born Sun, " Saturday Review, XXXV (September, 1952), 11-12.

Weeks, Donald. "Steinbeck Against Steinbeck, " The Pacific Spectator, I (Autumn, 1947), 447-457.

West, A. "Books; California Moonshine, " New Yorker, XXVIII (September 20, 1952), 121-122f.

Whipple, Leon. "Novels on Social Themes, " Survey Graphic, XXVIII (June, 1939), 401-402.

Whipple, Thomas King. "Steinbeck Through a Glass, Though Brightly, " New Republic, XCVI (October 12, 1938), 274-275.

Wilson, Edmund. "The Californians: Storm and Steinbeck, " New Republic, CIII (December 9, 1940), 784-787.

Wilson, Edmund. "I am Steinbeck's Newest Novel & James Joyce's First, " New Yorker, XX, January 6, 1945. 62.

Woodress, J. "John Steinbeck: Hostage to Fortune, " South Atlantic Quarterly, LXIII (Summer, 1964), 385-397.

Wright, Celeste Turner. "Ancient Analogues of an Incident in John Steinbeck, " Western Folklore, XIV

(January, 1955), 50-51.   (Analogues from Rome, Persia, etc. to sucking of old man in last chapter of The Grapes of Wrath.)

Young, Stark. "Serious Images," New Republic, CVI (May 11, 1942), 638-639.

Bombs Away (1942):

Book Reviews:

Graef, Richard. Catholic World, CLVI (February, 1943), 635.

Huie, William Bradford. Saturday Review of Literature, XXV (December 5, 1942), 22.

Langewiesche, Wolfgang. New York Herald Tribune Books, December 6, 1942. p. 3.

Prescott, Orville. New York Times, November 27, 1942. p. 21.

Williamson, S. T. New York Times Book Review, November 29, 1942. VI, pp. 1, 30.

Booklist, XXXIX (December 15, 1942), 132.

Library Journal, LXVIII (January 1, 1943), 37.

New Republic, CVIII (January 18, 1943), 94.

New York Herald Tribune Books, December 6, 1942. p. 3.

New Yorker, XVIII (November 28, 1942), 96.

Breakfast
French, Warren G. "Breakfast" in John Steinbeck. p. 81.

Sale, William, et al (eds.). "Breakfast," in Critical Discussions for Teachers Using Short Stories: Tradition & Direction. Norfolk, Conn.: New Directions, 1949. pp. 50-52.

Burning Bright (1950) (Novel)

Book Reviews:

Cousins, Norman. Saturday Review, XXXIII (October 28, 1950), 26-27.

Jackson, Joseph Henry. This World (San Francisco Chronicle), October 27, 1950. p. 16.

Kerr, Walter. The Commonweal, LIII (November 10, 1950), 120.

Larder, John. New Yorker, XXVI (October 28, 1950), 52-53.

Lockridge, Richard. New York Herald Tribune Books, October 22, 1950. p. 4.

Morris, Alice S. New York Times Book Review, October 22, 1950. VII, p. 4.

Prescott, Orville. New York Times, October 20, 1950, p. 25.

Wyatt, Euphemia Van Rensselaer. Catholic World, CLXXII (December, 1950), 228.

New York Times Book Review, VI, pp. 7, 26.

Newsweek, XXXVI (October 30, 1950), 78.

Theatre Arts, XXXIV (December, 1950), 16.

Time, LVI (October 30, 1950), 58.

Critical Essays:

Fontenrose, Joseph. "Burning Bright," in John Steinbeck: An Introduction & Interpretation. pp. 115-117.

French, Warren G. "Burning Bright," in John Steinbeck. pp. 148-152, 162-163, & Passim.

Geismar, Maxwell. "Burning Bright," in American Moderns, pp. 153-155.

Kennedy, John S. "Burning Bright," in SHC. pp. 131-133.

Lisca, Peter. "Burning Bright," in The Wide World of John Steinbeck. pp. 248-260.

Steinbeck, John. "Critics, Critics, Burning Bright," Saturday Review, XXXIII (November 11, 1950), 20-21.   Reprinted in Tedlock & Wicker (eds.) SHC. pp. 43-47.

Watt, F. W. "Burning Bright," in John Steinbeck. pp. 91-93.

Burning Bright (1951) (Play)
Atkinson, Brooks. New York Times, October 19, 1950. p. 40.

Atkinson, Brooks. New York Times Book Review, October 29, 1950. II, p. 1.

Geismar, Maxwell. Saturday Review of Literature, XXX (October 21, 1950), 14.

Goodman, Theodore R. New York Times Book Review, October 29, 1950. II, p. 3.

Kerr, Walter. Commonweal, LIII (November 10, 1950), 120.

Marshall, Margaret. Nation, CLXXI (October 28, 1950), 396.

Weiss, Carol H. Commonweal, LIII (November 24, 1950), 178.

Wyatt, Euphemia. The Catholic World, CLXXII (December, 1950), 228.

Zolotow, Sam. New York Times, October 27, 1950. p. 24.

Booklist, XLVII (September 1, 1950), 3.

Booklist, XLVII (November 1, 1950), 98.

Newsweek, XXXVI (October 30, 1950), 78.   A

musical by Richard Rodgers and Oscar Hammerstein II, based on Steinbeck's Play.

Nathan, G. J. "Burning Bright," in Theatre Book of the Year, 1950-1951, Toronto: MacClelland, 1952. pp. 67-70.

Weales, Gerald. "Steinbeck," in American Drama Since World War II. New York: Harcourt, Brace & World, Inc., 1962. pp. 198-199. (Burning Bright)

Cannery Row (1945)
Adams, J. Donald. New York Times Book Review, January 14, 1945. VII, p. 2.

Cousins, Norman. Saturday Review of Literature, XXVIII (March 17, 1945), 14.

Hampson, John. Spectator, CLXXV (November 2, 1945), 418-419.

Krutch, Joseph Wood. New York Herald Tribune Weekly Book Review, (December 31, 1955), p. 1.

Longaker, Mark. Catholic World, CLX (March, 1945), 570-571.

Marshall, Margaret. Nation, CLX (January 20, 1945), 75-76.

Matthiessen, F. O. New York Times Book Review, (December 31, 1944. VII, p. 1.

Mayberry, George. New Republic, CXII (January 15, 1945), 89-90.

Prescott, Orville. New York Times, January 2, 1945, p. 17.

Rothman, Nathan L. Saturday Review of Literature, XXVII (December 30, 1944), 5.

Toynbee, Philip. New Statesman & Nation, XXX (November 24, 1945), 356-357.

Wilson, Edmund. The New Yorker, XX (January 6,

1945), 62.

Wooster, Harold A. Library Journal, LXX (January 1, 1945), 32.

Booklist, XLI (January 1, 1945), 140.

Chicago Sun Book Week, (January 7, 1945.) p. 6.

Commonweal, XLI (January 26, 1945), 378.

Manchester Guardian, November 9, 1945. p. 3.

New Yorker, XX (January 6, 1945), 62.

Time, XLV (January 1, 1945), 62.

Times (London) Literary Supplement, November 3, 1945. p. 521.

Cooperman, Stanley. "Cannery Row, " in Review Notes & Study Guide to Steinbeck. pp. 62-75.

Fontenrose, Joseph. "Cannery Row, " in John Steinbeck: An Introduction & Interpretation. pp. 101-108.

French, Warren G. "Cannery Row, " in John Steinbeck, pp. 120-136, 139-141, 149-151, 157-158, 161-163, 166-169, & Passim.

French, Warren G. "Steinbeck, " in J. D. Salinger. New York: Twayne Publishers, Inc., 1963. pp. 43, 84, 106.
See II, B, 2.
See also The Pastures of Heaven and The Grapes of Wrath.

French, Warren G. "The Time the Wolves Ate the Vice-Principal, " (Possibly an inter-chapter omitted from Cannery Row, 1947). in John Steinbeck. pp. 129-131.

Gray, James. "Cannery Row, " in On Second Thought. pp. 137-139.

Jackson, Joseph Henry. "Introduction," in The Short
Novels of John Steinbeck. pp. xii-xiii (Cannery
Row)

"John Steinbeck Wins Back Rights to His Novel,
Cannery Row, from Producer B. Bryants," New
York Times, October 27, 1949. p. 38.
See II, A.

Kawamura, Yoneichi. "Steinbeck's Humor & Pathos
in Tortilla Flat & Cannery Row," Hokkaido University Essays in Foreign Languages & Literatures,
I (December, 1953), 24-30.
See Tortilla Flat.

Lisca, Peter. "Cannery Row," in The Wide World
of John Steinbeck. pp. 197-217.

Moore, Ward. "Cannery Row Revisited, Steinbeck
& The Sardine," Nation, **CLXXIX** (October 16,
1954), pp. 325-327.

Raymund, Bernard. "Cannery Row," in Writers of
Today. Ed. by Denys Val Baker. London:
Sidgwick, 1946. pp. 136-137.

Roane, Margaret C. "Cannery Row," in Wisconsin
Studies in Contemporary Literature, V (Summer,
1964), pp. 127-128.

Rothman, Nathan L. "A Small Miracle," Saturday
Review of Literature, **XXVII** (December 30, 1944),
5.   On Cannery Row.

Snell, George. "Cannery Row," in The Shapes of
American Fiction: 1798-1947. pp. 196-197.

Walcutt, Charles C. "Cannery Row," in American
Literary Naturalism. pp. 79-84.

Watt, F. W. "Cannery Row," in John Steinbeck.
pp. 79-84.

Chrysanthemums
   Beach, Joseph Warren. "Chrysanthemums," in
   American Fiction: 1920-1940. New York: Mac-
   millan, 1941. pp. 311-314. Also in SHC. pp.81-83.

Fontenrose, Joseph. "Chrysanthemums, " in John
Steinbeck. pp. 61-62.

French, Warren G. "The Chrysanthemums, " in John
Steinbeck. p. 83.

Kempton, Kenneth. "Chrysanthemums, " in Short
Stories for Study. Cambridge: Harvard University
Press, 1953. pp. 120-124.

Marcus, Mordecai. "The Lost Dream of Sex and
Childbirth in The Chrysanthemums, " MFS, XI
(Spring, 1965), 54-58.

Schramm, Wilber L. "The Chrysanthemums, " in
Fifty Best American Short Stories, 1915-1939.
Edited by Edward J. O'Brien. Boston: Houghton
Mifflin, 1939. pp. 925-927.

Simpson, Claude M. & Nelvin, Allan (eds.). "The
Chrysanthemums, " in The American Reader.
Boston: Heath, 1941. pp. 864-865.

Watt, F. W. "Chrysanthemums " in John Steinbeck.
pp. 42-44.

West, Roy B. , Jr. "Chrysanthemums, " in Short
Story in American, 1900-1950. Chicago: Henry
Regnery, 1952. pp. 48-49.

The Cup of Gold (1929)
Cuppy, Will. New York Herald Tribune Books,
August 18, 1939. p. 12.

Poor, Charles. New York Times, September 15,
1939. p. 27.

New York Evening Post, September 28, 1929. p. 7.

New York Evening Post, October 29, 1930. p. 7.

New York Herald Tribune Books, August 18, 1929.
p. 12.

Boynton, Percy. "Cup of Gold, " in America in
Contemporary Fiction. pp. 242-243.

Braley, Berton. "Acknowledgment (to John Steinbeck), " in Morgan Sails the Caribbean. New York: Macmillan, 1934. pp. vii-viii. The author explains his indebtedness to Steinbeck's Cup of Gold. See I, K.

Carpenter, Frederic I. "Cup of Gold, " in SHC. pp. 69-71.

Fontenrose, Joseph. "Cup of Gold, " in John Steinbeck: An Introduction & Interpretation. pp. 7-13.

French, Warren G. "Cup of Gold, " John Steinbeck. pp. 56-57 & Passim.

Gannett, Lewis. "John Steinbeck, " in Preface to The Cup of Gold, New York: Collier, 1936. pp. v-viii. See II, B, 1.

Gannett, Lewis. "Cup of Gold, " in John Steinbeck. pp. 9-10. See II, B, 1.

Geismar, Maxwell. "Cup of Gold, " in Writers in Crisis. pp. 246-248.

Lisca, Peter. "Cup of Gold, " in The Wide World of John Steinbeck. pp. 21-38. See II, B, 1.

Moore, Harry Thornton. "The Cup of Gold, " in The Novels of John Steinbeck: A First Critical Study. pp. 11-18.

Watt, F. W. "Cup of Gold, " in John Steinbeck. pp. 25-29.

"S. Bischoff Acquires Screen Rights to Book, Cup of Gold, " New York Times, December 16, 1945. II, p. 5. See II, A.

East of Eden (1952)
Brunn, Robert R. Christian Science Monitor, September 25, 1952. p. 11.

Chargnes, R. D. Spectator, CLXXXIX (November 28, 1952), 744.

Gurko, Leo. Nation, CLXXV (September 20, 1952), 235-236.

Hughes, Riley. Catholic World, CLXXVI (November, 1952), 150-151.

Jackson, Joseph Henry. This World (San Francisco Chronicle), September 21, 1952. p. 20.

Krutch, Joseph Wood. New York Herald Tribune Books, September 21, 1952. p. 1.

Magny, Claude-Edmonde. Perspective, November 5, 1953. Translated by Louise Varrese.

Mizener, Arthur. New Republic, CXXVII (October 6, 1952), 22-23.

Prescott, Orville. New York Times, September 19, 1952. p. 21.

Rolo, Charles. Atlantic, CXC (October, 1952), 94.

Schorer, Mark. New York Times Book Review, September 21, 1952. VII, p. 1.

Scott, J. D. New Statesman of Nation, IV (December 6, 1952), 698-699.

Smith, Eleanor Touhey. Library Journal, LXXVII (August, 1952), 1303.

Varrese, Louise (translator).
See Magny, Claude-Edmonde --- East of Eden --- Book Review Section.

Webster, Harvey Curtis, and Kolb, Bernard.
Saturday Review, XXXV (September 20, 1952), 11-12.

West, Anthony. New Yorker, XXVIII (September 20, 1952), 111-113.

Booklist, XLVIII (July 15, 1952), 369.

Booklist, XLIX (September 19, 1952), 33.

Bookmark, XII (October, 1952), 10.

Christian Science Monitor, September 25, 1952. p. 11.

Manchester Guardian, December 5, 1952. p. 4.

Time, LX (September 22, 1952), 110.

Times (London) Literary Supplement, December 5, 1952. p. 789.

Yale Review, XLII (Autumn, 1962), 8.

Cooperman, Stanley. "East of Eden, " in Review Notes & Study Guides. pp. 76-95.

"East of Eden, a best-seller," Facts on File, XII (October 31-November 6, 1952), 355.
See II, A.

"East of Eden, a movie, was produced by Warner Bros. , " Facts on File, XV (April 7-13, 1955), 127.
See II, A.

Fontenrose, Joseph. "East of Eden, " in John Steinbeck: An Introduction & Interpretation. pp. 118-127.

Frohock, W. M. "East of Eden," in The Novel of Violence in America. pp. 141-143.

French, Warren G. "East of Eden, " in John Steinbeck, pp. 152-156, & Passim.

Fuller, Edmund. "East of Eden" in Man in Modern Fiction. New York: Random House, 1958. pp. 25-29.

Gardiner, Harold Charles. "Novelist to Philosopher?" in In All Conscience; Reflections on Books & Culture. Garden City, N. Y. : Hanover House, 1959. pp. 136-138. (East of Eden).
See II, B, 2.

Geismar, Maxwell. "East of Eden, " in American Moderns. pp. 164-167.

Hobson, L. Z. "Trade Winds, " Saturday Review, XXXV (August 30, 1952), 4.

Krutch, Joseph Wood. "East of Eden, " in SHC. pp. 302-305. Also in "John Steinbeck's Dramatic Tale of Three Generations, " New York Times Book Review, September 21, 1955.

Leonard, Frank G. "East of Eden, " in "Cozzens Without Sex; Steinbeck Without Sin, " Antioch Review, XVIII (Summer, 1958), 209-218.

Lewis, R. W. B. "East of Eden, " in "John Steinbeck: The Fitful Daemon, " in The Young Rebel in American Literature. Editor Carl Bode. London: Heineman, 1959. pp. 131-134.

Lisca, Peter. "East of Eden, " in The Wide World of John Steinbeck. pp. 261-275.

Magny, Claude-Edmonde. "John Steinbeck's East of Eden, " Perspective USA, V (Fall, 1953), 146-152.

Mizener, Arthur. "East of Eden" in "Does a Moral Vision of the Thirties Deserve a Nobel Prize?" New York Times Book Review, December 9, 1962. pp. 43-44.

Osborn, Paul (ed.). "Dialogue Script; East of Eden, " Study of Current English (Tokyo), X (September, 1955), 16-32.

Phillips, William. "Male-ism and Moralism: Hemingway & Steinbeck, " American Mercury, LXXV (October, 1952), 93-98.   (East of Eden)

Sawey, Orlan. "Another Logic at East of Eden, Appalachian State Teachers College Faculty Publications (Formerly ASTC Bulletin), (N. V.), 1964. 54-58.

Watt, F. W. "East of Eden, " in John Steinbeck. pp. 93-99.

Webster, Harvey Curtis. "Out of the New-born Sun, "
Saturday Review, XXXV (September 20, 1952),
11-12.

Flight
Antico, John. "A Reading of Steinbeck's Flight, "
MFS, XI (Spring, 1965), 45-53.

French, Warren G. "Flight, " in John Steinbeck. pp.
119, 141-142.

Friedman, Norman. " 'Flight': What Makes a Short
Story Short?" Modern Fiction Studies, IV
(Summer, 1958), 113-114.

Havighurst, Walter. "Flight, " in Instructor's Manual
for Masters of the Modern Short Story. New York:
Harcourt, Brace, 1945. pp. viii-ix.

Jones, William M. "Steinbeck's 'Flight, ' "
Explicator, XVIII (November, 1959), Item 11.

Lisca, Peter. "Flight, " in The Wide World of John
Steinbeck. pp. 98-100.

Madeo, Frederick. " 'Flight' --- An Allegorical
Journey, " English Record, XIV (April, 1964),
55-58.

Roane, Margaret C. "Flight, " in Wisconsin Studies
in Contemporary Literature, V (Summer, 1964),
pp. 129-130.

Vogel, Dann. "Steinbeck's 'Flight': The Myth of
Manhood, " College English, XXIII (December,
1961), pp. 225-226. Reply by C. F. Chapin.
College English XXIII (May, 1962), 676.

Watt, F. W. "Flight, " in John Steinbeck. pp. 45-46.

Wills, Arthur. "A Question of Manhood: Steinbeck's
'Flight', " Exercise Exchange, XII (November,
1964), 14-15.

The Forgotten Village (1941)
Crandell, R. F. New York Herald Tribune Books,
June 1, 1941. p. 6.

Fairley, Barker. Canadian Forum, XXI (August, 1941), 153.

Hartung, Philip T. Commonweal, XXXIV (July 25, 1941), 329-330.

Marshall, Margaret. Nation, CLIII (July 12, 1941), 36.

Thompson, Ralph. New York Times, May 26, 1941. p. 17.

Booklist, XXXVII (July 1, 1941), 513.

New York Herald Tribune Books, June 1, 1941. p. 6.

New York Times Book Review, June 1, 1941. VI, pp. 8, 18.

New Yorker, XVII (June 7, 1941), 77.

Time, XXXVII (June 2, 1941), 88.

French, Warren G. "The Forgotten Village," in John Steinbeck. pp. 26, 86, 96, 114, 116, 147.

"New York Censors Ban The Forgotten Village," Time, XXXVIII (September 1, 1941), 54. See IV.

"Producer-Director of The Forgotten Village," Time, XXXVIII (December 8, 1941), 96.

The Gift (See The Red Pony.)

The Grapes of Wrath (1939)
Angoff, Charles. North American Review, CCXLVII (Summer, 1939), 387.

Birney, Earl. Canadian Forum, XIX (June, 1939), 94-95.

Caskey, J. Homer. Saturday Review of Literature, XX (May 20, 1939), 9.   A Letter.

Cowley, Malcolm. New Republic, XCVIII (May 3,

1939), 382-383.

Fadiman, Clifton. New Yorker, XV (April 15, 1939), 81.

Jack, Peter Monro. New York Times Book Review, April 16, 1939. VII, p. 2.

Jackson, Joseph Henry. New York Herald Tribune Books, April 16, 1939. p. 3.

Kronenberger, Louis. Nation, CXLVIII (April 15, 1939), 440-441.

Kuhl, Art. Catholic World, CL (November, 1939), 160-165.

O'Brien, Kate. Spectator, CLXIII (September 15, 1939), 386.

Poore, Charles. New York Time, April 14, 1939. p. 27.

Stevens, George. Saturday Review of Literature, XIX (April 15, 1939), 3.

Thompson, Ralph. Yale Review, XXVIII (Summer, 1939), viii.

Vaughan, James N. Commonweal, XXX (July 28, 1939), 341-342.

Weeks, Edward. Atlantic, CLXIII (April, 1939), p. 591; (May, 1939), 734.

West, Anthony. New Statesman & Nation, XVIII (September 16, 1939), 404-405.

Booklist, XXXV (April 15, 1939), 271.

Christian Science Monitor, May 6, 1939. p. 13.

Forum, CII (July, 1939), p. 4.

Manchester Guardian, September 8, 1939. p. 3.

New York Herald Tribune Books, April 16, 1939. p. 3.

New Yorker, XV (April 15, 1939), 101.

Time, XXXIII (April 17, 1939), 87.

Time, XXXV (February 12, 1940), 70.

Times (London) Literary Supplement, September 9, 1939. p. 525.

Wilson Library Bulletin, XXXV (May, 1939), 104.

Allen, Walter. "The Grapes of Wrath," in Tradition & Dream: The English & American Novel From the Twenties and Our Time. London: Phoenix House, 1963. pp. 164-166; Also in The Modern Novel in Britain & The United States. New York: Dutton, 1964.

"Associated Farmers of Keru County, California, Approve Ban on The Grapes of Wrath," Wilson Library Bulletin, XIV (October, 1939), 102.

"Attempts to Suppress The Grapes of Wrath," Publishers' Weekly, CXXXVI (September 2, 1939), 777.

Baker, Carlos. "The Grapes of Wrath," in "Steinbeck of California," Delphian Quarterly, XXIII (April, 1940), pp. 43-44.

Baker, Howard. "The Grapes of Wrath," in "In Praise of the Novel," Southern Review, V (1940), 787-790.   (The Fiction of Huxley, Steinbeck, et al.)

Beach, Joseph Warren. "The Grapes of Wrath," American Fiction, 1920-1940. New York: Macmillan, 1942. pp. 327-347; Also in SHC, pp. 250-265.

Bennett, Robert. The Wrath of John Steinbeck, or Saint John Goes to Church. Los Angeles: Albertson Press, 1939. (Pamphlet). Also in The Monthly Record, (N. V.) (June, 1950), (N. P.)
See II, B, 1.

Birney, Earle. "The Grapes of Wrath," Canadian

Forum, **XIX** (June, 1939), 94.

Bluestone, George. "The Grapes of Wrath," in Novel Into Film. Baltimore: Johns Hopkins University Press, 1957. pp. 147-169, 211. Also in A Companion to The Grapes of Wrath. Edited by Warren G. French.

Boren, Lyle. U. S. Congressional Record Appendix, 76th Congress, 3rd Session, 1944. LXXXVI, Part 13, 139-140. (A Comment on The Grapes of Wrath).

Bowden, Edwin T. "The Grapes of Wrath," in The Dungeon of The Heart: Human Isolation and the American Novel. New York: Macmillan, 1961. pp. 138-149.

Bowron, Bernard. "The Grapes of Wrath: A 'Wagons West' Romance," Colorado Quarterly, III (Summer, 1954), 84-91. (Much of the appeal of the novel is that it largely follows the "Covered Wagon" romance formula. --- PMCA.)

Boynton, Percy. "The Grapes of Wrath," in America in Contemporary Fiction. University of Chicago Press, 1940. pp. 251-257.

Brown, Deming. "The Grapes of Wrath," in Soviet Attitudes Toward American Writing. Princeton University Press, 1962. pp. 74-80, 139-140, 162-164, 177-178, & Passim.

Burgum, Edwin Berry. "The Grapes of Wrath," The Novel & The World's Dilemma. New York: Oxford University Press, 1947. pp. 283-288; Also in SHC, pp. 112-116.

Brynes, Asher. "A Man Who Lived With Failure," New Republic, CXLV (August 21, 1961), 24. See also The Winter of our Discontent.

Burbank, Rex. "In Dubious Battle" and The Grapes of Wrath" in Thornton Wilder. New York: Twayne, 1961. pp. 79-80.

California Citizens Association Report. "Was The

Grapes of Wrath Answered?" in A Companion to
The Grapes of Wrath. Edited by Warren French.
pp. 138-139.

Canby, Henry Seidel. "The Right Question," Saturday Review of Literature, XXI (March 23, 1940),
8.

Cannon, F. "Pauline Apostleship of Tom Joad,"
College English, XXIV (December, 1962),
222-224. On The Grapes of Wrath.

Carlson, Eric W. "Symbolism in The Grapes of
Wrath," College English, XIX (January, 1958),
172-175.

Carpenter, Frederick I. "John Steinbeck: The
Philosophical Joads," in American Literature &
the Dream. New York: Philosophical Library,
1955. pp. 167-175. Also in "John Steinbeck: The
Philosophical Joads," College English, II
(January, 1941), 315-325;   Also in SHC, pp.
241-249.

Carpenter, Frederick I. "Philosophical Joads,"
College English, II (January, 1941), pp. 315-325.
(Also in Steinbeck and His Critics. Edited by
Ernest W. Tedlock, Jr. & C. V. Wicker. pp.
241-249.

Casimir, Louis, Jr., Jr. "The Grapes of Wrath:
They Just Kept Rolling Along," in "Human
Emotion & the Early Novels of John Steinbeck,"
Unpublished dissertation, the University of Okla-
homa, 1965. Chapter VII.

Caughey, John Walton. "Current Discussion of
California's Migrant Labor Problem," Pacific
Historical Review, VIII (September, 1939),
347-354. (The Grapes of Wrath).

Chametzky, Jules. "The Ambivalent Endings of The
Grapes of Wrath," MFS, XI (Spring, 1965),
34-44.

"Christian Symbolism in The Grapes of Wrath:
Discussion," College English, XIX (January,

1958), 172-175; (May, 1958), 369.

Condon, F. "Grapes of Raps; Hollywood Makes a Picture, Strictly Under Blankets," Collier's, CV (January 27, 1940), 23ff.

Cooperman, Stanley. "The Grapes of Wrath," in Review Notes & Study Guide to Steinbeck. pp. 41-61.

Crockett, H. Kelly. "Bible and The Grapes of Wrath," College English, XXIV (December, 1962), 193-199. Reply with Rejoinder by T. F. Dunn, College English, XXIV (April, 1963), 566-567.

De Schweinitz, George. "Steinbeck & Christianity," College English, XIX (May, 1958), 369. "The Grapes of Wrath."

Detweiler, Robert. "Christ and the Christ Figure in American Fiction," Christian Scholar, XLVII (Summer, 1964), 111-124. "The Grapes of Wrath."

Dougherty, Charles, T. "Christ Figure in The Grapes of Wrath," College English, XXIV (December, 1962), 224-226.

Dunn, Thomas F. "The Grapes of Wrath," College English, XXIV (April, 1963), 566-567.

Eisinger, Chester E. "Jeffersonian Agrarianism in The Grapes of Wrath," The University of Kansas City Review, XIV (Winter, 1947), 149-154.

Fairley, Barker. "John Steinbeck of the Coming Literature," Sewanee Review, L (April-June, 1942), 145-161.

"La Follett Committee Investigation Based on The Grapes of Wrath," Time, XXXIV (August 21, 1939), 10.
See II, A.

Fontenrose, Joseph. "The Grapes of Wrath," in John Steinbeck: An Introduction & Interpretation. pp. 67-83.

French, Warren G. "L'Affaire Lettuceberg" (Early working title of The Grapes of Wrath, " in John Steinbeck.) p. 24.

French, Warren G. "Another Look At The Grapes of Wrath, " Colorado Quarterly, III (Winter, 1955), 337-343.

French, Warren G. (ed.). A Companion to The Grapes of Wrath. New York: Viking Press, 1963. See II, B, 1.

French, Warren G. "The Grapes of Wrath, " in John Steinbeck. pp. 25-26, 72-73, 95-112, 140-142, 146-147, 149-150, 151-152, 172-173, & Passim.

French, Warren G. John Steinbeck. New York: Twayne Publishers, Inc., 1961. U. S. Authors Series.
See II, B, 1.

French, Warren G. "Steinbeck, " (The Grapes of Wrath, Cannery Row, The Pastures of Heaven) in J. D. Salinger. New York: Twayne Publishers, Inc., 1963. pp. 43, 84, 106.
See II, B, 2.
See also Cannery Row; The Pastures of Heaven.

Frohock, W. M. "The Grapes of Wrath, " in The Novel of Violence in America. pp. 129-133.

Geismar, Maxwell David. "John Steinbeck: Of Wrath or Joy, " in Writers in Crisis: The American Novels, 1925-1940. Boston: Houghton Mifflin, 1942. pp. 237-270.
See II, B, 2.

"German Documents Reveal That Hitler Cited the Novel, The Grapes of Wrath as Example of Living Conditions in U. S., " New York Times, April 8, 1947. p. 13.

Goethals, Thomas R. The Grapes of Wrath: A Critical Commentary. New York: R. D. M. Corporation, 1963.
See II, B, 1.

"The Grapes of Wrath, " in American Writing Today. pp. 398-399.

"The Grapes of Wrath, " Collier's, CIV (September 2, 1939), 54.

"The Grapes of Wrath: Career, " New York Times, May 7, 1940. pp. 20, 24.

"The Grapes of Wrath: Cited in Article on California Migratory Labor, " New York Times, August 27, 1939. VII, p. 10.

"The Grapes of Wrath Cited in P. V. McNutt Article, " New York Times, March 17, 1942. VII, p. 12.

"The Grapes Has First Birthday, " Publishers' Weekly, CXXXVII (April 13, 1940), 1493-1494. (The Grapes of Wrath).
See II, A.

"The Grapes of War: S. Prose from England, " Newsweek, XXII (July 5, 1943), 94-96.
See II, A.

"The Grapes of Wrath: Association of Farmers of Kern County Seeks California Ban, " New York Times, August 23, 1939. p. 17.
See II, A.

"The Grapes of Wrath Banned By Buffalo Library, " Publishers' Weekly, CXXXVI (August 12, 1930), 453.
See II, A.

"The Grapes of Wrath Banned in Kansas City, " New York Times, August 19, 1939. p. 8.
See II, A.

"The Grapes of Wrath Consigned to Flames By Library Board of East St. Louis, Illinois, " Publishers' Weekly, CXXXVI (November 25, 1939), 1994.
See II, A.

"The Grapes of Wrath: East St. Louis Library

109

Orders Copies of The Grapes of Wrath Burned,"
New York Times, November 15, 1939. p. 21.
See II, A.

"The Grapes of Wrath Gets New Sales Stimulus,"
Publishers' Weekly, CXXXVI (December 30, 1939),
2320.
See II, A.

"The Grapes of Wrath: He Gives Pulitzer Prize
Checks to R. Lovejoy for Literary Career, New
York Times, June 16, 1940. p. 3.
See II, A.

"The Grapes of Wrath: He Wins American Best-
sellers Association Award," New York Times,
February 14, 1940. p. 19.
See II, A.

"The Grapes of Wrath: He Wins Pulitzer Prize,"
New York Times, May 7, 1940. p. 1.
See II, A.

"The Grapes of Wrath: He Wins Social Work Today
Award," New York Times, April 2, 1940. p. 28.
See II, A.

"The Grapes of Wrath: Mrs. F. D. Roosevelt Holds
He Did Not Exaggerate," New York Times,
April 3, 1940. p. 25.
See II, A.

"The Grapes of Wrath: Mrs. Roosevelt Comments
on the Book," New York Times, December 8,
1939. p. 16.
See II, A.

"The Grapes of Wrath: Praised by Pearl Buck,"
New York Times, November 30, 1939. p. 18.
See II, A.

"The Grapes of Wrath: Screen Rights Sold," New
York Times, April 21, 1939. p. 21.
See II, A.

"The Grapes of Wrath To Be Published," New York
Times, January 11, 1943. p. 2.

See II, A.

"The Grapes of Wrath: To Collaborate with H. Kleine on Film Production," New York Times, April 7, 1940. IX, p. 5. See II, A.

Gray, James. "The Grapes of Wrath," in On Second Thought. pp. 134-136.

Griffin, R. J. and Freedman, W. A. "Machines and Animals: Pervasive Motifs in The Grapes of Wrath," Journal of English and German Philology, LXII (July, 1963), 569-580.

Gurko, Leo. "The Joads in California," in The Angry Decade. New York: Dodd, Mead, 1947. pp. 201-221.

Hartrangt, Marshall V. Grapes of Gladness. Los Angeles: DeVorss & Co., 1939. (California's refreshing & inspiring answer to John Steinbeck's Grapes of Wrath, with extracts from the reviews of The Grapes of Wrath by Burton Rascoe, John D. Barry, & Thomas W. McManns.) See II, A.; II, B, 1.

Hartt, Julian N. "The Grapes of Wrath," in The Lost Image of Man. Baton Rouge: Louisiana State University Press, 1964. pp. 74-76.

Hayashi, Tetsumaro. "John Steinbeck's The Grapes of Wrath: The Joad Clan and Women," Lumina, IV (1961), 1-4.

Hoffman, Frederick J. "The Grapes of Wrath," in The Modern Novel in America, 1900-1950. Chicago: Regnery, 1960. pp. 165-168.

Hunter, F. P. "Steinbeck's Wine of Affirmation in The Grapes of Wrath," in Essays in Modern American Literature. Edited by Richard E. Langford & Guy Owen. DeLand, Florida: Stetson University Press, 1963. pp. 76-89.

Hunter, J. Paul. "Steinbeck's Wine of Affirmation in The Grapes of Wrath," Stetson Studies in the

Humanities, I (1961), 76-89.

Isherwood, Christopher. "The Tragedy of Eldorado,"
Kenyon Review, I (Autumn, 1939), 450-453.

Jackson, Joseph Henry. "Introduction" to The Grapes
of Wrath. New York: Limited Edition Club &
Heritage Press, 1940.
See II, B, 2.

Jackson, Joseph Henry. Why Steinbeck Wrote 'The
Grapes of Wrath,' New York: Limited Editions
Club, 1940.
See II, B, 1.

Kazumi, Kazushi. "Notes on The Grapes of Wrath,"
English & American Literature Study, Aoyama
Gakuin University, VIII (February, 1962), 1-17.

Kennendy, John S. "The Grapes of Wrath," Fifty
Years of the American Novel. Edited by Harold
C. Gardiner. New York: Scribner's, 1951.
Passim.

Klammer, Enno. "The Grapes of Wrath - A Modern
Exodus Account," Cresset, XXV (February, 1962),
8-11.

Knitz, S. J. "The Grapes of Wrath," Wilson
Library Bulletin, XIV (October, 1939), 102, 165.

Kronenberger, Louis. "The Grapes of Wrath," in
College Prose. pp. 424-427.

Kuhl, A. "Mostly of The Grapes of Wrath,"
Catholic World, CL (November, 1939), 160-165.

Kuhl, A. "Mostly of The Grapes of Wrath,"
Catholic World, CL (November, 1939), 160-165.

Kunitz, Stanley J. "Wine Out of These Grapes,"
Wilson Library Bulletin, XIV (October, 1939), 165.

Kuzumi, Kuzushi. "Notes on The Grapes of Wrath,"
Aoyama Gakuin University Studies in British &
American Literature, VIII (1962), 1-17.

Lawson, John Howard. "The Grapes of Wrath," in
Film: The Creative Process. New York: Hill &
Wang, 1964. pp. 215-218, 358.

"Letter on the Ban of the Grapes of Wrath," New
York Times, November 17, 1939. p. 20.
See II, A.

Lisca, Peter. "The Grapes of Wrath," in The Wide
World of John Steinbeck. pp. 144-177.

Lisca, Peter. "The Grapes of Wrath As Fiction,"
PMLA, LXXII (March, 1957), 296-309.

Long, Louise. "The Grapes of Wrath," Southwest
Review, XXIV (July, 1939), 495-498.

Longstreet, Stephen. "The Grapes of Wrath," in
College Prose, pp. 428-430.

McEldery, B. R., Jr. "The Grapes of Wrath in
the Light of Modern Critical Theory," College
English, V (March, 1964), 308-313. Reprinted in
French (ed.), Companion to The Grapes of Wrath,
pp. 199-208.

McWilliams, Carey. "What's Being Done About The
Goods?," New Republic, C (September 20, 1939),
178-180. On The Grapes of Wrath.

McEldery, B. R. Jr., "The Grapes of Wrath in the
Light of Modern Critical Theory," College English,
V (March, 1944), 308-313.

Matsutori, Mataki. "John Steinbeck: All That Lives
Is Holy," Kyashu Institute of Technology Report,
VIII (March, 1960), 1-6.

Miron, George Thomas. The Truth About John Steinbeck & The Migrants. Los Angeles: Haynes Corp.,
1939.
See II, B, 1.

Mizener, Arthur. "The Grapes of Wrath," New York
Times Book Review, December 9, 1952. pp. 44-45.

"Mrs. Roosevelt Comments on The Grapes of Wrath,"

Time, XXXV (April 15, 1940), 17.
See II, A.

Monroe, N. Elizabeth. "The Grapes of Wrath," in
The Novel and Society. Chapel Hill: University
of North Carolina Press, 1941. pp. 17-18 &
Passim.

Moore, Harry Thornton. "The Grapes of Wrath,"
in The Novels of John Steinbeck, pp. 54-72.

"More Wrath; 'Phony Pathos' in Writings Flayed
(Letter)," Time, XXXV (March 25, 1940), 14.
See II, B, 3.

Morris, Lloyd. "The Grapes of Wrath," in Postscript to Yesterday. New York: Random House,
1947. pp. 167-171.

Moseley, Edwin M. "Christ as the Brother of Man:
Steinbeck's The Grapes of Wrath," in Pseudonyms
of Christ in the Modern Novel: Motifs & Methods.
University of Pittsburgh Press, 1963, pp. 163-175.

Nye, Russel B. "The Grapes of Wrath - an Analysis,"
in Civilization, Past & Present, Edited by T.
Walter Thompson & Alastair M. Taylor. Chicago:
Scott, Foresman & Co., 1961. II, pp. 564-565.

"Original Typescript of Book, The Grapes of Wrath
Given to The Library of Congress," New York
Times, December 25, 1941, p. 31.
See II, A.

"Original Typescript of Book, The Grapes of Wrath,
discussed," New York Times, February 1, 1942.
VI, p. 22.

Orlova, R. "Money Against Humanity: Notes on the
Work of John Steinbeck," Tr. Armin Moskovic,
in A Companion to The Grapes of Wrath. Edited
Warren French. pp. 152-159.

Orvis, Mary. "The Grapes of Wrath," in The Art
of Writing Fiction, New York: Prentice-Hall,
1948. pp. 196-200.

Pollock, Theodore. "On The Ending of The Grapes of Wrath," Modern Fiction Studies, IV (Summer, 1958), 177-178.

Poore, Charles. "Introduction," in The Grapes of Wrath. New York: Harper's Modern Classics, 1951. pp. vii-xv.

Raymund, Bernard. "The Grapes of Wrath," in Writers of Today. pp. 127-136.

"Red Meat & Red Herrings; Excerpt from Reviews of The Grapes of Wrath," Commonweal, XXX (October 13, 1939), 562-563.

Rundell, Walter, Jr. "The Grapes of Wrath," in "Steinbeck's Image of the West," The American West, I (Spring, 1964), pp. 4-8 & Passim.

Saw, Sally. "Religious Symbols in Steinbeck's Grapes," The Joad Newsletter, I (January, 1963), 1-2.

Shockley, Martin Staples. "Christian Symbolism in The Grapes of Wrath," College English, XVIII (November, 1956), 87-90. Also in Steinbeck and His Critics. Edited by Ernest W. Tedlock, Jr., & C. V. Wicker. pp. 266-274.

Shockley, Martin Staples. "The Reception of The Grapes of Wrath in Oklahoma," American Literature, XV (January, 1944), 351-361. Also in Steinbeck and His Critics. Edited by Ernest Tedlock, Jr., and C. V. Wicker. pp. 231-240.

Sillen, Samuel. "Censoring The Grapes of Wrath," New Masses, XXXII (September 12, 1939), 23-24.

Slochower, Harry. "The Grapes of Wrath," in No Voice is Wholly Lost. pp. 299-306.

Slochower, Harry. "The Promise of America: John Steinbeck." Literature and Philosophy Between Two World Wars: The Problem in a War Culture. New York: Citadel Press, 1964. Passim.

Snell, George. "The Grapes of Wrath," in The

Shapes of American Fiction: 1798-1947. pp. 193-196.

Stevens, George. "Steinbeck's Uncovered Wagon," Saturday Review of Literature, XIX (April 15, 1939), 3-4.

Stovall, Floyd. "The Grapes of Wrath," American Idealism. Norman: University of Oklahoma Press, 1943. pp. 159-166.

Taylor, F. J. "California's Grapes of Wrath; Joad Family Not Typical," Forum, CII (November, 1939), 232-238. Abridged in Reader's Digest, XXXV (November, 1939), 89-95. Discussion in Forum, CII (December, 1939), Supp. 7; CIII (January, 1940), 24-25.

Taylor, Walter Fuller. "The Grapes of Wrath Reconsidered," Mississippi Quarterly, XII (Summer, 1959), 136-144.

Tedlock, E. W., Jr. & C. V. Wicker (eds.). Steinbeck and His Critics. pp. xxxii-xxxv.

Times (London) Literary Supplement. "The Grapes of Wrath," in American Writing Today: Its Independence and Vigor. New York: University Press, 1957. pp. 398-399.

Tuttleton, James W. "The Grapes of Wrath," "Steinbeck in Russia: The Thetoric of Praise & Blame," MFS, XI (Spring, 1965), Passim.

Tyler, Parker. "The Grapes of Wrath," in Magic and Myth of the Movies. New York: Henry Holt, 1947. pp. 230-247, 274-278.

Uzzell, Thomas H. "The Grapes of Wrath," in The Technique of the Novel. New York: Citadel Press, 1964. pp. 231 & Passim.
See II, B, 2.

Van Doren, Carl. "The Grapes of Wrath," in The American Novel, 1789-1939. New York: Macmillan, 1940. pp. 364-366.

Van Doren, Carl Clinton. "Introduction" to The
  Grapes of Wrath. Cleveland: World Publishing
  Co., 1947.
  See II, B, 2.

"Vestal High School, Vestal, N. Y. Has Faculty &
  Students Defy Harold C. May, The President of
  The Board of Education, & Put Steinbeck's The
  Grapes of Wrath & Salinger's The Catcher in The
  Rye on Sale Despite The Board Action," New
  York Times, March 28, 1965. p. 76.
  See II, A.

Watt, F. W. "The Grapes of Wrath," in John Steinbeck. pp. 63-75.

Weeks, E. A. "The Grapes of Wrath," in Essays
  For Our Time. Edited by A. L. Boder & C. F.
  Wells. (n. p., n. d.), pp. 226-228.

Westwood, Horace. "The Grapes of Wrath," Unity,
  CXXIV (February 5, 1940), 170-173.

Whicher, George F. "Proletarian Learnings," in
  The Literature of American People. Edited by
  Arthur Hobson Quinn. New York: Appleton-
  Century-Crofts, 1951. pp. 958-961. "The Grapes
  of Wrath"

Wilson, Edmund. "The Grapes of Wrath," Classics
  & Commercials. pp. 38-42.

Wright, Celester T. "Ancient Analogues of an
  Incident in John Steinbeck" Western Folklore,
  XIV (January, 1955), 50-51.

Yoshida, Hiroshige. "Gender of Animation in John
  Steinbeck's The Grapes of Wrath," Anglica, II
  (October, 1956), 106-122.

The Great Mountain   See The Red Pony.

The Harness
  French, Warren G. "The Harness," in John Steinbeck. pp. 83-84.

How Mr. Hogan Robbed a Bank
    French, Warren G. "How Mr. Hogan Robbed a
    Bank, " in John Steinbeck. pp. 30, 170-171,
    (manuscript play), 171.

In Dubious Battle (1936)
    Baker, Carlos. New York Times, July 25, 1943.
    pp. 4, 16.

    Benét, William Rose. Saturday Review of Literature,
    XIII (February 1, 1936), 10.

    Chamberlain, John. Current History, XLIII (March,
    1936), iv.

    McCarthy, Mary. Nation, CXLII (March 11, 1936),
    326-327.

    Moore, Harry Thornton. New Republic, LXXXVI
    (February 19, 1936), 54.

    Poore, Charles. New York Times, September 15,
    1939. p. 27.

    Quennell, Peter. New Statesman & Nation, XI
    (May 2, 1936), 670.

    Smith, Bernard. New York Herald Tribune Books,
    February 2, 1936. p. 6.

    Tompkins, Lucy. New York Times, February 2,
    1936. p. 7.

    New York Herald Tribune Books, February 2, 1936.
    p. 6.

    Literary Digest, CXXI (February 1, 1963), 28.

    Spectator, CLVI (May 8, 1936), 850.

    Times (London) Literary Supplement, May 16, 1936.
    p. 417.

    Allen, Walter. "In Dubious Battle, " in Tradition &
    Dream. pp. 161-162.

Baker, Carlos. "In Dubious Battle Revalued," New York Times Book Review, July 25, 1943. pp. 4, 16.

Blotner, Joseph L. "John Steinbeck: The Party Organizer," in The Political Novel. Garden City, N.Y.: Doubleday, 1955. p. 14.
See II, B, 2.

Burbank, Rex. "In Dubious Battle" & "The Grapes of Wrath," in Thornton Wilder. New York: Twayne, 1961. pp. 79-80.

Casimir, Louis J., Jr. "In Dubious Battle: True Wars Are Never Won," in "Human Emotions and the Early Novels of John Steinbeck," Unpublished dissertation, The University of Oklahoma, 1965. "Chapter IV"

De Voto, Bernard. "Dubious Battle in California," Nation, CXLIII (September 12, 1936), 302-304.

"Dubious Battle in California," Nation, CXLIII (September 12, 1936), 302-304. On In Dubious Battle.

Fontenrose, Joseph. "In Dubious Battle," in John Steinbeck. pp. 42-53.

French, Warren G. "In Dubious Battle," in John Steinbeck. pp. 62-71, 149-150, & Passim.

Frohock, W. M. "In Dubious Battle," The Novel of Violence in America. pp. 134-137.

Gannett, Louis. "In Dubious Battle," in John Steinbeck: Personal & Bibliographical Notes. pp. 13-14.

Geismar, Maxwell. "In Dubious Battle," in Writers in Crisis: The American Novels Between Two Wars. Boston: Houghton Mifflin. 1942. pp. 260-263.

Hartt, Julian N. "In Dubious Battle," in The Lost Image of Man. Baton Rouge: Louisiana State University Press, 1964. pp. 74-76.

Jackson, Joseph Henry. "Introduction" to The Short
Novels of John Steinbeck. New York: Viking Press,
1963. pp. ix-x.

Levant, Howard Stanley. "The Unity of In Dubious
Battle: Violence and Dehumanization, " MFS, XI
(Spring, 1965), 21-33.

Lisca, Peter. "In Dubious Battle, " pp. 108-129.

Mizener, Arthur. "In Dubious Battle, " New York
Times Book Review, December 9, 1962. pp. 4,
43.

Moore, Harry Thornton. "In Dubious Battle, " in
The Novels of John Steinbeck. pp. 41-47.

Nakachi, Akira. "The Grapes of Wrath: A Novel of
Mankind, " Taira Technical Junior College Reports
of Study, I (1961), 1-15.

Walcutt, Charles C. "In Dubious Battle, " in American Literary Naturalism, A Divided Stream.
Minneapolis: University of Minnesota Press, 1956.
pp. 260-262.

Watt, F. W. "In Dubious Battle, " in John Steinbeck.
Evergreen Pilot Books. New York: Grove Press,
1962. pp. 51-58.

Whipple, Thomas K. "In Dubious Battle, " in Study
Out The Land. Berkeley: University of California
Press, 1943. pp. 109-110.

Johnny Bear
French, Warren G. "Johnny Bear, " in John Steinbeck. pp. 85-86.

The Leader of the People
Clough, Wilson O. "The Leader of the People, " in
The Necessary Earth: Nature & Solitude in
American Literature. Austin: University of Texas
Press, 1964. pp. 148-149.

French, Warren G. "The Leader of the People, " in
John Steinbeck. pp. 92-94.

Grommon, Alfred H. "Who Is The 'Leader of the People?' Helping Students Examine Fiction," English Journal, XLVIII (November, 1959), 449-456.

Hogopian, John V. & Martin Dolch. "The Leader of the People," in Insight I: Analysis of American Literature. Frankfurt Am. Main: Hirschgroben-Verlog, 1962. pp. 230-235.

Jaffe, Adrian H. & Virgil Scott. "The Leader of the People," in Studies In The Short Story. New York: Dryden, 1947. pp. 172-181.

Lisca, Peter. "The Leader of the People," in The Wide World of John Steinbeck. pp. 104-107.

Ross, Woodburn O. & A. Doyle Wallace. "The Leader of the People," in Short Stories in Context. New York: American Book Company, 1953. pp. 16-19.

Short, Raymond & Sewall, Richard B. "The Leader of the People," in A Manual For Teachers Using "Short Story For Study." New York: Holt, 1960. pp. 16-17; 3rd ed., 1956. pp. 1-2.

The Log From The Sea Of Cortez   See Sea of Cortez.

The Long Valley (1938)
Davis, Elmer. Saturday Review of Literature, XVIII (September 24, 1938), 11.

Soskin, William. New York Herald Tribune Books, September 18, 1938. p. 7.

Thompson, Ralph. New York Times, September 21, 1938. p. 29.

Thompson, Ralph. Yale Review, XXVIII (Winter, 1939), X.

Walter, Eda Lou.   Nation, CXLVII (October 1, 1938), 331-332.

Young, Stanley. New York Times Book Review, September 25, 1938. p. 7.

Booklist, XXXV (October 1, 1938), 48.

New York Herald Tribune Books, September 18, 1938. p. 7.

New Yorker, XIV (September 24, 1938), 92.

Fontenrose, Joseph. "Torgas Valley & Long Valley," in John Steinbeck: An Introduction & Interpretation. pp. 42-66.

French, Warren G. "The Long Valley," in John Steinbeck. pp. 25, 80-94.

Lisca, Peter. "The Long Valley," in The Wide World of John Steinbeck. pp. 92-107.

"The Viking Press Buys Contract, Orders for The Long Valley Earnings," Time, XXXII (August 29, 1938), 47.
See II, A.

The Moon Is Down (1942) (Novel)
Butler, E. M. Catholic World, CLV (May, 1942), 253-254.

Chamberlain, John. New York Times, March 6, 1942. p. 19.

Cousins, Norman. Saturday Review of Literature, XXV (March 14, 1942), 6.

Duffus, R. C. New York Times Book Review, March 8, 1942. VI, pp. 1, 27.

Duffy, Charles. Commonweal, XXXV (March 27, 1942), 569-570.

Fadiman, Clifton. New Yorker, XVIII (March 7, 1942), 52.

Garrison, W. W. Christian Century, LIX (April 29, 1942), 561-562.

Gassner, John. Current History, II (May, 1942), 228.

Gunther, John. New York Herald Tribune Books, March 8, 1942. p. 1.

Krutch, Joseph Wood. The Nation, CXLV (December 11, 1937), 663.

Marshall, Margaret. Nation, CLIV (March 7, 1942), 286.

O'Brien, Kate. Spectator, CLXIX (July 10, 1942), 44.

Stegner, Wallace. Boston Globe, March 11, 1942. p. 19.

Thurber, James. The New Republic, CVI (March 16, 1942), 370.

Toynbee, Philip. New Statesman & Nation, XXIII (June 20, 1942), 408-409.

Weeks, Donald. Atlantic Monthly, CLXIX (April, 1942), (n. p. , Between 398-399)

Young, Stark. The New Republic, CVI (May 11, 1942), 638.

Booklist, XXXVIII (March 15, 1942), 252.

Bookmark, III (May, 1942), 17.

Catholic World, CLV (May, 1942), 253.

Christian Science Monitor, March 6, 1942. p. 18.

Library Journal, LXVII (February 15, 1942), 182.

Life, XII (April 6, 1942), 32-34.

Manchester Guardian, June 26, 1942. p. 3.

New York Herald Tribune Books, March 8, 1942. p. 1.

New Yorker, XVIII (March 7, 1942), 59; XVIII (April 4, 1942), 63.

Newsweek, XIX (April 20, 1942), 72.

Time, XXXIV (March 9, 1942), 84.

Times (London) Literary Supplement, June 20, 1942. p. 305.

Yale Review, XXXI (Spring, 1942), 8.

"Article on Russian Review of Moon Is Down, " New York Times, December 22, 1942. p. 23.

"Belgian Information Center Issued Bill of Complaints (on Moon Is Down, " New York Times, April 28, 1942. p. 19.

Burgum, Edwin Berry. "The Moon Is Down, " in Tedlock & Wicker (eds.). SHC. pp. 116-118.

Eisinger, Chester E. "The Moon Is Down, " in Fiction Of The Forties. University of Chicago Press, 1963. pp. 50-51, 100-101.

Fontenrose, Joseph. "The Moon Is Down, " in John Steinbeck: An Introduction & Interpretation. pp. 98-101.

French, Warren G. "The Moon Is Down, " in John Steinbeck. pp. 113-119, 149-150, & Passim.

"Gets Norwegian Award for Moon Is Down, " New York Times, January 21, 1947. p. 21. See II, A.

Hyman, Stanley Edgar. "Some Notes on John Steinbeck; New Transition in The Moon Is Down; with Reply By P. Bixler, " Antioch Review, II (June, 1942), 185-200; 322-323. Also in Steinbeck and His Critics. Edited by Edgar W. Tedlock, Jr., & C. V. Wicker. pp. 152-166.

Jackson, Joseph Henry. "The Moon Is Down, " in "Introduction" to The Short Novels of John Steinbeck. pp. xi-xii.

"Letter on The Moon Is Down, " New York Times, April 5, 1942. VI, p. 2.

Lisca, Peter. "The Moon Is Down," in The Wide World of John Steinbeck. pp. 191-196.

"Moon Is Halfway Down," New Republic, CVI (May 18, 1942), 657.

Watt, F. W. "The Moon Is Down," in John Steinbeck. Evergreen Pilot Books. pp. 77-79.

The Moon Is Down: A Play In Two Parts (1943).
Adey, Alvin. Current History, II (April, 1942), 143-144.

Burnham, David. Commonweal, XXXVI (April 24, 1942), 14.

Gassner, John. Current History, II (May, 1942), 228-232.

Gilder, Rosamond. Theatre Arts, XXVI (May, 1942), 287.

Thurber, James. New Republic, CVI (March 16, 1942), 370.

Wyatt, Euphemia. Catholic World, CLV (May, 1942), 213-214.

Young, Stark. New Republic, CVI (May 11, 1942), 638.

Library Journal, LXVII (September 1, 1942), 739.

New York Times, November 15, 1963. p. 5.

Theatre Arts, XXVI (May, 1942), 287.

Time, XXXIX (April 20, 1942), 36.

Time, XXXIX (June 22, 1942), 88.

"Biggest Cinema Story Price," Time, XXXIX (May 11, 1942), 47. (The Moon Is Down)
See II, A.

Gassner, John. " 'The Moon Is Down' as a Play. "

Current History, New Series II (May, 1942), 228-231.

Gilder, Rosamond. "Moon Down. Theatre Rises." Theatre Arts, XXVI (May, 1942), 287-289.

"The Moon Is Down Opens in Stockholm," Time, XLI (April 19, 1943), 42.
See II, A.

The Murder
French, Warren G. "The Murder," in John Steinbeck. pp. 22, 86-87.

Nothing So Monstrous
French, Warren G. "Nothing So Monstrous," (Chapter from The Pastures of Heaven with an epilogue, 1936), in John Steinbeck. p. 43.

Of Mice & Men (1937) (Novel)
Canby, Henry S. Saturday Review of Literature, XV (February 27, 1937), 7.

Paul, Louis. New York Herald Tribune Books, February 28, 1937.

Thompson, Ralph. New York Times, February 27, 1937. p. 15.

Thompson, Ralph. New York Times, March 2, 1937. p. 19.

Van Doren, Mark. Nation, CXLIV (March 6, 1937), 275.

Van Doren, Mark. Nation, CXLIV (April 18, 1942), 468.

Walton, Eda Lou. New York Times Book Review, February 28, 1937. VII, pp. 7, 20.

Weeks, Donald. Atlantic Monthly, CLIX (April, 1937), (n. p. : between 384-385).

Wyatt, Euphemia. Catholic World, CXLVI (January, 1938), 468-469.

Young, Stark. New Republic, XCIII (December 15, 1937), 170-171.

Commonweal, XXVII (December 10, 1937), 191.

Literary Digest, CXXIV (December 18, 1937), 34.

Newsweek, IX (February 27, 1937), 39.

Theatre Arts, XXI (October, 1937), 774-781.

Theatre Arts, XXII (January, 1938), 13-16.

Time, XXIX (March 1, 1937), 69.

Time, XXX (December 6, 1937), 41.

Allen, Walter. "Of Mice & Men," in Tradition & Dream. pp. 163-164.

Baker, Carlos. "Of Mice & Men," in "Steinbeck of California," Delphian Quarterly, XXIII (April, 1940), 42.

Boynton, Percy. "Of Mice & Men," in America In Contemporary Fiction. pp. 248-250.

Burgum, Edwin Berry. "Of Mice & Men," in Tedlock & Wicker (eds.), SHC. pp. 109-112.

Carpenter, Frederic I. "Of Mice & Men," in Tedlock & Wicker (eds.), SHC. pp. 76-77.

Casimir, Louis J., Jr. "Of Mice & Men: St. George & The Reluctant Dragon," Unpublished dissertation, The University of Oklahoma, 1965. "Chapter V"

Cooperman, Stanley. "Of Mice & Men," in Review Notes & Study Guide to Steinbeck. pp. 25-40.

Dusenbury, Winifred L. "Steinbeck: Of Mice & Men," in The Themes of Loneliness in Modern American Drama. Gainesville: University of Florida Press, 1960. pp. 45-50.

127

Fontenrose, Joseph. "Of Mice & Men, " in John
Steinbeck. pp. 53-59.

French, Warren G. "Of Mice & Men, " in John
Steinbeck. pp. 72-79, 149-150, & Passim. Play,
1937, pp. 24, 27, 76. Film, 1941. p. 24.

Geismar, Maxwell. "Of Mice & Men, " in Writers
in Crisis. pp. 256-260.

Ganapathy, R. "Steinbeck's Of Mice & Men: A
Study of Lyricism Through Primitivism" Literary
Criterion, V (Winter, 1962), 101-104.

Jackson, Joseph Henry. "Introduction, " to Of Mice
& Men. New York: Random House, Modern
Library, 1937.
See II, B, 2.

Lisca, Peter. "Motif and Pattern in Of Mice And
Men, " Modern Fiction Studies, II (Winter, 1956),
228-234.

Lisca, Peter. "Of Mice & Men, " in The Wide World
of John Steinbeck. pp. 130-143.

Moore, Harry Thornton. "Of Mice & Men, " in The
Novels of John Steinbeck. pp. 47-54.

"Of Mice & Men: Criticism, " Life & Letters Today,
XXII (July, 1939), 93-94.

"Of Mice & Men. Criticism, " New Statesman &
Nation, XVII (April 22, 1939), 605-608.

"Of Mice & Men. Criticism, " Spectator, CLXII
(April 21, 1939), 668.

Rascoe, Burton. "Of Mice & Men, " English Journal,
XXVII (March, 1938), Passim.

Raymund, Bernard. "Of Mice & Men, " Writers of
Today. p. 127.

Roane, Margaret C. "Of Mice & Men, " Wisconsin
Studies in Contemporary Literature. V (Summer,
1964). p. 130.

Van Doren, Mark. "Wrong Number," in The
Private Reader. New York: Holt, 1942. pp. 255-
257.

Of Mice and Men: A Play in Three Acts (1937)
Atkinson, Brooks. New York Times, November 24,
1937. p. 20.

Atkinson, Brooks. New York Times Book Review,
December 12, 1937. XI, p. 3.

Calta, Louis. New York Times, December 5, 1958.
p. 38. Musical version.

Issacs, Edith J.R. Theatre Arts, XXII (January,
1938), 13-16.

Krutch, Joseph Wood. Nation, CXLV (December 11,
1937), 663-664.

Vernon, Grenville. Commonweal, XXVIII (June 3,
1938), 161.

Wyatt, Euphemia Van Reusselaer. Catholic World,
CXLVI (January, 1938), 468.

Young, Stark. New Republic, XCIII (December 15,
1937), 170.

Literary Digest, CXXIV (December 18, 1937), 34.

Atkinson, Brooks. "Of Mice & Men," in Broadway
Scrapbook. New York: Theatre Arts, Inc., 1947.

Brown, John Mason. "Mr. Steinbeck's Of Mice &
Men," in Two On the Aisle; Ten Years of the
American Theatre in Performance. New York:
W. W. Norton, 1938. pp. 183-187.
See II, B, 2.

French, Warren G. "The First Theatrical Productions of Steinbeck's Of Mice and Men," American
Literature, XXXVI (January, 1965), 525-527.

Isaacs, Edith J.R. "Of Mice & Men," Theatre Arts
Anthology. New York: Theatre Arts Books, 1950.

pp. 644-646.

Mantle, Robert Burns. "Of Mice & Men," in
Contemporary American Playwrights. New York:
Dodd, Mead, 1938. pp. 3-6.

"Of Mice & Men (Play): Feature & Article," New
York Times, April 24, 1938. X, p. 1.

"Of Mice & Men (Play): G. George Comments,"
New York Times, April 24, 1938. X, p. 1.

"Of Mice & Men (Play): New York Drama Critics
Circle Award Presented," New York Times,
April 25, 1938. p. 19.

"Of Mice & Men (Play): Steinbeck Interviewed,"
New York Times, December 5, 1937. p. 7.
See II, A.

"Of Mice & Men (Play) Receives Critics Award,"
Time, XXXI (April 25, 1938), 39.
See II, A.

"Of Mice & Men (Play) Wins New York Drama
Critics Circle Award," New York Times, April
19, 1938. p. 23.
See II, A.

Shedd, Margaret. "Of Mice & Men," Theatre Arts,
XVII (October, 1937), 774-778.

Once There Was A War (1958)
French, Warren G. "Once There Was a War," in
John Steinbeck. pp. 27, 86.

Houlihan, T. Library Journal, LXXXIII (September
15, 1958), 2436.

Mitgang, Herbert. New York Times Book Review,
November 16, 1958. VII, p. 12.

Swinton, Stan. Saturday Review, XLI (November 1,
1958), 18.

Booklist, LV (September 1, 1958), 8; (November 1,
1958), 122.

Chicago Sunday Tribune, October 26, 1958. p. 10.

Christian Science Monitor, October 17, 1958. p. 9.

New York Herald Tribune Book Review, February 8, 1959. p. 10.

New Yorker, XXXIV (November 8, 1958), p. 203.

San Francisco Chronicle, October 17, 1958. p. 33.

The Times (London) Literary Supplement, January 8, 1900. p. 15.

The Pastures of Heaven (1932)
Abels, Cyrilly. Bookman, LXXV (December, 1932), 877-878.

Dawson, Margaret C. New York Herald Tribune Books, October 23, 1932. p. 2.

Mofett, Anita. New York Times, November 20, 1932. pp. 5, 16, 20.

Booklist, XXIX (December, 1932), 116.

Chicago Daily Tribune, November 19, 1932. p. 14.

Nation, CXXXV (December 7, 1932), 574.

New York Evening Post, October 29, 1930, p. 3.

New York Herald Tribune Books, October 23, 1932, p. 2.

Saturday Review of Literature, IX (November 26, 1932), 275-276.

Yale Review, XXII (Winter, 1933), 22.

Boynton, Percy. "The Pastures of Heaven," in America In Contemporary Fiction. pp. 244-246.

Carpenter, Frederic I. "The Pastures of Heaven," in Tedlock & Wicker (eds.), SHC. pp. 71-73.

Casimir, Louis J., Jr. "The Pastures of Heaven:
There are Serpents in Paradise," in "Human
Emotions & The Early Novels of John Steinbeck,"
Unpublished dissertation, The University of Okla-
homa, 1965. "Chapter II"

Fontenrose, Joseph. "The Pastures of Heaven," in
John Steinbeck: An Introduction & Interpretation.
pp. 20-29.

French, Warren G. "The Pastures of Heaven," in
John Steinbeck. pp. 39-46, 146-147, & Passim.

French, Warren G. "Steinbeck," (The Grapes of
Wrath, Cannery Row, The Pastures of Heaven) in
J. D. Salinger, New York: Twayne Publishers,
Inc., 1963. pp. 43-84, 106.
See II, B, 2; See The Grapes of Wrath; Cannery
Row.

Geismar, Maxwell. "The Pastures of Heaven," in
Writers in Crisis. pp. 242-246.

Lisca, Peter. "The Pastures of Heaven," in The
Wide World of John Steinbeck, pp. 56-71.

Mizener, Arthur. "The Pastures of Heaven," in
New York Times Book Review, December 9, 1962.
p. 4.

Moore, Harry Thornton. "The Pastures of Heaven,"
in The Novels of John Steinbeck. pp. 19-23.

Snell, George. "The Pastures of Heaven," in The
Shapers of American Fiction: 1798-1947. pp.
190-191.

Watt, F. W. "The Pastures of Heaven," in John
Steinbeck. pp. 33-37.

The Pearl (1947)
Baker, Carlos. New York Times Book Review,
November 30, 1947. VII, p. 4.

Farrelly, John. New Republic CXVII (December 23,
1947), 28.

Geismar, Maxwell. Saturday Review of Literature, XXX (November 22, 1947), 14.

Hunter, Anne. Commonweal, XLVII (January 23, 1948), 377.

Kingery, Robert E. Library Journal, (November 1, 1947), 1540.

Prescott, Orville. New York Times, November 24, 1947. p. 21.

Sugrue, Thomas. New York Herald Tribune, December 7, 1947. p. 4.

Weeks, Edward. Atlantic, CLXXX (December, 1947), 138-139.

Booklist, XLIV (December 15, 1947), 152.

Chicago Sun Book Week, November 23, 1947, p. 7.

New Yorker, XXIII (December 27, 1947), 59.

Newsweek, XXXI (March 8, 1948), 83-84.

San Francisco Chronicle, December 14, 1947, p. 16.

Time, L (December 22, 1947), 90.

Time, LI (March 1, 1948), 84.

Cooperman, Stanley. "The Pearl," in Review Notes & Study Guide to Steinbeck. New York: Monarch Press, 1964. pp. 16-24.

Corin, Fernand. "Steinbeck & Hemingway: A Study in Literary Economy," Revue Des Langues Vivantes, XXIV (January-February & March-April, 1958), 60-75, 153-163.

Fontenrose, Joseph. "The Pearl," in John Steinbeck: An Introduction & Interpretation. pp. 111-114.

French, Warren G. "The Pearl," in John Steinbeck. p. 137-142, & Passim.

Fuller, Edward. "Afterward," in his & Blanche Jennings Thompson (eds.), Four Novels For Appreciation. New York: Harcourt, Brace, 1960. pp. 656-660.

Geismar, Maxwell. "The Pearl," in American Moderns. pp. 151-153.

Hatch, R. L. "The Pearl, A Screen Play," New Republic, CXVIII (March 1, 1948), 26.

Jackson, Joseph Henry. "Introduction," The Short Novels of John Steinbeck. pp. xiii-xiv. (The Pearl).

Karsten, Ernest E., Jr. "Thematic Structure in The Pearl," English Journal, LIV (January, 1965), 1-7.

Lisca, Peter. "The Pearl," in The Wide World of John Steinbeck. pp. 218-230. Also in Tedlock & Wicker (eds.), SHC., pp. 291-301.

Morris, H. "The Pearl: Realism and Allegory," English Journal, LII (October, 1963), 487-495, 503.

Morris, Harry. "The Pearl: Realism & Allegory" in Scholarly Appraisals of Literary Works Taught In High Schools, Edited by National Council of Teachers of English. Champaign, Illinois: NCTE, 1965. p. 83. (A Selected Bibliography for Steinbeck's The Pearl.)

Tuttleton, James W. "The Pearl," in "Steinbeck in Russia: The Rhetoric of Praise & Blame," MFS, XI (Spring, 1965), pp. 85-86.

Watt, F. W. "The Pearl," in John Steinbeck. pp. 84-87.

The Promise   See The Red Pony.
French, Warren G. "The Promise," in John Steinbeck. pp. 91-92.

The Raid
French, Warren G. "The Raid," in John Steinbeck.

p. 80.

The Red Pony: I. The Gift II. The Great Mountain
III. The Promise (1937) IV. The Leader
of the People (1945).

Thompson, Ralph. New York Times, September 29,
1937. p. 21.

Walton, Edith H. New York Times Book Review,
October 10, 1937. VII, p. 7.

Chicago Sun Book Week, September 16, 1945. p. 2.

The Red Pony (1937)
Thompson, Ralph. New York Times, September 29,
1937. p. 21.

Walton, Edith H. New York Times Book Review,
October 10, 1937. VII, p. 7.

Chicago Sun Book Week, September 16, 1945. p. 2.

New York Herald Tribune Books, November 4, 1945.
p. 6.

Time, XXX (October 11, 1937), 79.

Carpenter, Frederick I. "The Red Pony, " in SHC,
pp. 77-78.

Casimir, Louis J. , Jr. "The Red Pony and the
Black Stallion: Love and Death in the American
Bildungsroman, " in "Human Emotion and the Early
Novels of John Steinbeck, " Unpublished disserta-
tion, University of Oklahoma, 1965. Chapter VI.

Fontenrose, Joseph. "The Red Pony, " in John Steinbeck. pp. 63-66.

French, Warren G. "The Gift, " in John Steinbeck.
pp. 89-90.

_____. "The Great Mountain, " in John Stein-
beck. pp. 90-91.

135

_____ . "The Red Pony, " in John Steinbeck. pp. 89-94, Passim.

Gierasch, Walter. "Steinbeck's 'The Red Pony II': 'The Great Mountains, " Explicator, IV (1946), Item 39.

Goldsmith, Arnold L. "Thematic Rhythm in The Red Pony, " College English, XXVI (February, 1965), 391-394.

Heiney, Donald W. "The Red Pony, " in Recent American Literature. Great Neck, N. Y. : Barron, 1958. pp. 234-235.

Jackson, Joseph Henry. "The Red Pony, " in Introduction to The Short Novels of John Steinbeck. p. xi.

Lisca, Peter. "The Red Pony, " in The Wide World of John Steinbeck. pp. 100-104.

Mizener, Arthur. "The Red Pony, " in New York Times Book Review, December 9, 1962. p. 4.

Moore, Harry Thornton. "The Pony, " in The Novels of John Steinbeck. pp. 33-35.

"The Red Pony, a Screen Play, " Good Housekeeping, CXXVII (December, 1948), 198.

Reich, Charles R. "Study Questions for The Red Pony, " Excercise Exchange, IX (April, 1962), 3-4.

Singleton, Ralph H. "The Red Pony, " in Instructor's Manual For Two and Twenty: A Collection of Short Stories. New York: St. Martin's Press, 1962. pp. 13-14.

Watt, F. W. "The Red Pony, " in John Steinbeck. pp. 46-49.

A Russian Journal (1948)
Adams, Scott. Library Journal, LXXIII (April 15, 1948), 658.

Atkinson, Oriana. New York Times Book Review,

May 9, 1948. VII, p. 3.

Barry, Iris. New York Herald Tribune Books, April 18, 1948. p. 3.

Fischer, Louis. Saturday Review of Literature, XXXI (May 15, 1948), 13.

French, Warren G. "A Russian Journal, " in John Steinbeck. pp. 28-69.

Jackson, Joseph Henry. This World (San Francisco Chronicle), April 18, 1948. p. 14.

Prescott, Orville. New York Times, April 16, 1948. p. 21.

Watts, Richard, Jr. New Republic, CXVIII (April 19, 1948), 22-23.

Booklist, XLIV (May 15, 1948), 311.

New Yorker, XXIV (May 1, 1948), 91.

Time, LI (January 26, 1948), 58.

St. Katy, the Virgin
French, Warren G. "St. Katy, the Virgin, " in John Steinbeck. pp. 80, 87-88, 121.

Sea of Cortez with Edward F. Ricketts (1941):
Doughty, Howard H. , Jr. New York Herald Tribune Books, December 7, 1941. p. 3.

Duffus, R. L. New York Times Book Review, December 28, 1941. VI, p. 3.

Fadiman, Clifton. New Yorker, XVII (December 6, 1941), 133.

Gilroy, Harry. New York Times Book Review, September 16, 1951. VII, p. 6.

Hart, Eugene D. Library Journal, LXVI (October 15, 1941), 903.

Hyman, Stanley Edgar. New Republic, CVI (February

16, 1942), 242.

Munz, Charles Curtis. Nation, CLIII (December 20, 1941), 647.

Peattie, Donald Culross. Saturday Review of Literature, XXIV (December 27, 1941), 5.

Poore, Charles. New York Times, September 22, 1951. p. 15.

Poore, Charles. New York Times, December 5, 1941. p. 21.

Roth, Claire, J. Library Journal, LXXVI (October 1, 1951), 1565-1566.

Booklist, XXXVIII (January 1, 1942), 153.

Booklist, XLVIII (October 15, 1951), 68.

New Yorker, XVII (December 6, 1941), 133.

New Yorker, XXVII (October 6, 1951), 125-126.

New York Herald Tribune Books, December 7, 1941. p. 3.

Time, XXXVIII (December 22, 1941), 64.

Fontenrose, Joseph. "Sea of Cortez," in John Steinbeck. pp. 84-97.

French, Warren G. "Log From The Sea of Cortez," in John Steinbeck. pp. 29-172.

_____. "Sea of Cortez," in John Steinbeck. Preface, pp. 26, 28, 138.

Lisca, Peter. "Sea of Cortez," in The Wide World of John Steinbeck. pp. 178-185.

The Short Reign of Pippin IV: A Fabrication (1957):
B., A. Canadian Forum, XXXVII (July, 1957), 89.

Bois, William. New York Times, April 15, 1957.

p. 27.

George, Daniel. Spectator, CXCVIII (May 31, 1957), 726-727.

Hughes, Riley. Catholic World, CLXXXV (July, 1957), 312.

Janeway, Elizabeth. New York Times Book Review, April 14, 1957. VII, p. 6.

Johnson, Pamela Hansford. New Statesman, LIV (July 13, 1957), 61-62.

Moore, Harry T. New Republic, CXXXVI (May 27, 1957), 23-24.

Ray, David. Nation, CLXXXIV (April 20, 1957), 346-347.

Redman, Ben Ray. Saturday Review, XL (April 13, 1957), 14.

Smith, Eleanor T. Library Journal, LXXXII (March 15, 1957), 753.

Weeks, Edward. Atlantic, CC (July, 1957), 83-84.

Booklist, LIII (March 1, 1957), 345.

Booklist, LIII (April 15, 1957), 428.

Bookmark, XVI (May, 1957), 191.

Manchester Guardian, June 4, 1957), p. 4.

New Yorker, XXXIII (April 13, 1957), 164.

Time, LXIX (April 15, 1957), 15.

Times (London) Literary Supplement, June 7, 1957. p. 345.

Fontenrose, Joseph. "The Short Reign of Pippin IV," in John Steinbeck. pp. 130-132.

French, Warren G. "Short Reign of Pippin IV, " in
John Steinbeck. pp. 30, 111, 165-169.

Geismar, Maxwell. "The Short Reign of Pippin IV, "
in American Moderns. pp. 155-156.

"If I Were King, " Time, LXIX (April 15, 1957), 126.

Lisca, Peter. "The Short Reign of Pippin IV, " in
The Wide World of John Steinbeck. pp. 284-288.

Ray, David. "Many Keys to Steinbeck, " Nation,
CLXXXIV (April 20, 1957), 346-347.

"The Short Reign of Pippin IV, " Library Journal,
LXXXII (March 15, 1957), 753.

Watt, F. W. "The Short Reign of Pippin IV, " in
John Steinbeck. pp. 101-102.

The Snake
French, Warren G. "The Snake, " in John Steinbeck.
pp. 22, 80, 81-82, 119, 157.

Greet, T. Y. , et al (eds.). "The Snake, " in The
World of Fiction: Stories in Context. Boston:
Houghton Mifflin, 1964. pp. 370-375.

Sweet Thursday (1954)
Gill, Brendan. New Yorker, XXX (July, 1954), 63-64.

Baker, Carlos. New York Times Book Review, June
13, 1954. VII, p. 4.

Barron, Louis. Library Journal, LXXIX (June 1,
1954), 1052.

Boyle, Robert H. Commonweal, LX (July 9, 1954),
351.

Holman, Hugh. New Republic, CXXX (June 7, 1954),
18-20.

Hughes, Riley. Catholic World, CLXXIX (April, 1954),
393-394.

Poore, Charles. New York Times, June 10, 1954.

p. 29.

Richardson, Maurice. New Statesman and Nation, XLVIII (November 6, 1954), 589-590.

Rugoff, Milton. New York Herald Tribune Books, June 13, 1954. p. 1.

Webster, Harvey Curtis. Saturday Review, XXXVII (June 12, 1954), 11.

Weeks, Edward. Atlantic, CXCIV (August, 1954), 82.

Booklist, L (April 15, 1954), 309; L (June 15, 1954), 401.

Manchester Guardian, October 26, 1954. p. 4.

Nation, CLXXIX (July 10, 1954), 37.

New Yorker, XXX (July 10, 1954), 63.

Time, LXIII (June 14, 1954), 120-121.

Times (London) Literary Supplement, November 26, 1954. p. 753.

Fontenrose, Jospeh. "Sweet Thursday," in John Steinbeck. pp. 127-130.

French, Warren G. "Sweet Thursday," in John Steinbeck. pp. 156-160, 162-163, Passim.

Holman, C. Hugh. "Sweet Thursday," in "A Narrow-Gauge Dickens," New Republic, CXXX (June 7, 1954), 18-20.

Lisca, Peter. "Sweet Thursday," in The Wide World of John Steinbeck. pp. 276-284.

Metzger, Charles R. "Steinbeck's Version of the Pastoral," Modern Fiction Studies, VI (Summer, 1960), 115-124.

Watt, F. W. "Sweet Thursday," in John Steinbeck. pp. 99-101.

Their Blood Is Strong
    French, Warren G. "Their Blood Is Strong," in
    John Steinbeck. pp. 25-87.

To a God Unknown (1933)
    Barney, Virginia. New York Times Book Review,
    October 1, 1933. p. 18.

    Dawson, Margaret C. New York Herald Tribune
    Books, September 24, 1933. p. 17.

    S., C. Saturday Review of Literature, X (October
    28, 1933), 224.

    Christian Century, L (September 20, 1933), 1179.

    Forum, XC (November, 1933), viii.

    Nation, CXXXVII (October 18, 1933), 456.

    New Republic, LXXVII (December 20, 1933), 178.

    New York Herald Tribune Books, September 24,
    1933. p. 17.

    New York Times, October 1, 1933. p. 18.

    Boynton, Percy. "To a God Unknown," in America
    in Contemporary Fiction. pp. 244-246.

    Carpenter, Frederick K. "To a God Unknown," in
    SHC. pp. 73-74.

    Fontenrose, Joseph. "To a God Unknown," in John
    Steinbeck. pp. 13-19.

    French, Warren G. "To a God Unknown," in John
    Steinbeck. pp. 47-52, Passim.

    Geismar, Maxwell. "To a God Unknown," in
    Writers in Crisis. pp. 248-252.

    Lisca, Peter. "To a God Unknown," in The Wide
    World of John Steinbeck. pp. 39-55.

    Moore, Harry T. "To a God Unknown," in The
    Novels of John Steinbeck. pp. 23-33.

Ross, Woodburn, O. "To a God Unknown," in "John
Steinbeck: Earth and Stars," in SHC. pp. 172-173.
Also in University of Missouri Studies in Honor
of A. H. R. Fairchild, Ed. by Charles T. Prouty.
Columbia, Mo.: University of Missouri Press,
1946.

Shimada, Saburo. "A Study of John Steinbeck's To
A God Unknown," Beacon Study in English Language and Literature, V (1964), 23-25.

Snell, George. "To a God Unknown," in The Shapes
of American Fiction: 1798-1947. pp. 189-190.

Uchida, Shigeharu. "John Steinbeck's Non-Teleology
and To a God Unknown," Kyushu American Literature, VI (April, 1963), 13-17.

Watt, F. W. "To a God Unknown," in John Steinbeck.
pp. 29-33.

Tortilla Flat (1935)
Benet, William Rose. Saturday Review of Literature,
XII (June 1, 1935), 12.

Chamberlain, John. Current History, XLII (July,
1935), 7.

Colby, Harriet. New York Herald Tribune Books,
June 2, 1935. p. 4.

Mangione, Jerre. New Republic, LXXXIII (July 13,
1935), 285.

Marsh, Fred T. New York Times, June 2, 1935.
p. 6.

Neville, Helen. Nation, CXL (June 19, 1935), 720.

Chicago Daily Tribune, June 1, 1935. p. 14.

New York Herald Tribune Books, June 2, 1935. p. 4.

Saturday Review (London), CLX (November 23, 1935),
501.

Spectator, CLV (December 6, 1935), 960.

Time, XXXIX (May 18, 1942), 84.

Times (London) Literary Supplement, December 21, 1935. p. 877.

Baker, Carlos. "Tortilla Flat," in "Steinbeck of California," Delphian Quarterly, XXIII (April, 1940), 41-42.

Beach, Joseph Warren. "Tortilla Flat," in American Fiction, 1920-1940. pp. 317-322.

Carpenter, Frederick I. "Tortilla Flat," in SHC. pp. 74-75.

Casimir, Louis J., Jr. "Tortilla Flat: A Funny Story But Not Pleasant to Laught At," in his Ph. D. dissertation. Chapter II.

Fontenrose, Joseph. "Tortilla Flat," in John Steinbeck. pp. 30-41.

French, Warren G. "Tortilla Flat," in John Steinbeck. pp. 22-23, 53-61, Passim. Preface to Modern Library Edition, p. 54; Play, p. 24. Film, p. 23.

Geismar, Maxwell. "Tortilla Flat," in Writers in Crisis. pp. 252-256.

Gibbs, Lincoln R. "Tortilla Flat," in SHC. pp. 95-97.

Jackson, Joseph Henry. "Tortilla Flat," in Introduction to The Short Novels of John Steinbeck. pp. viii-ix.

Kawamura, Yoneichi. "Steinbeck's Humor and Pathos in Tortilla Flat and Cannery Row," Hokkaido University Essays in Foreign Languages and Literature, I (December, 1953), 24-30.
See also Cannery Row.

Kinney, Arthur F. "The Arthurian Cycle in Tortilla Flat," Modern Fiction Studies, XI (Spring, 1965), 11-20.

144

Lisca, Peter. "Tortilla Flat," in The Wide World of John Steinbeck. pp. 72-91.

Moore, Harry T. "Tortilla Flat," in The Novels of John Steinbeck. pp. 35-41.

Raymund, Bernard. "Tortilla Flat," in Writers of Today. London: Sidgwicker, 1946. pp. 125-127.

Roane, Margaret C. 'Tortilla Flat," in Wisconsin Studies in Contemporary Literature, V (Summer, 1964), 129.

Snell, George. "Tortilla Flat," in The Shapes of American Fiction: 1798-1947). pp. 191-192.

Uchida, Shigeharu. "Sentimental Steinbeck and His Tortilla Flat," Kyushu American Literature, VII (1964), 8-12.

Watt, F. W. "Tortilla Flat," in John Steinbeck. pp. 37-42.

Travels With Charles in Search of America (1962)
Brown, John Mason. Book-of-the-Month Club News, XXXV (Midsummer, 1962), 1.

Butcher, Fanny. Chicago Sunday Tribune Magazine of Books. July 29, 1962. p. 1.

Gannett, Lewis. New York Herald Tribune Books, July 29, 1962. p. 3.

Gerber, Rudolph J. America, CVII (August 4, 1962), 569.

Goldman, Eric F. New York Times Book Review, July 29, 1962. VII, p. 5.

Hogan William. San Francisco Sunday Chronicle ("This World Magazine"), July 29, 1962. p. 24.

Moon, Eric. Library Journal, LXXXVII (June 15, 1962), 2378.

Pickrel, Paul. Harper's, CCXXV (August, 1962), 91.

Prescott, Orville. New York Times, July 27, 1962. p. 23.

Rivers, William. Saturday Review, XLV (September 1, 1962), 31.

Weeks, Edward. Atlantic, CCX (August, 1962), 138.

Wallaston, Nicholas. Spectator, CCIX (October 19, 1962), 604-605.

Booklist, LVIII (July 1, 1962), 748; LVIII (July 15, 1962), 784.

Christian Science Monitor, August 2, 1962. p. 7.

Holiday, XXXII (August, 1962), 13.

New Yorker, XXXVIII (September 8, 1962), 152.

Newsweek, LX (July 30, 1962), 77.

Time, LXXX (August 10, 1962), 70.

Times (London) Literary Supplement, November 2, 1962. p. 843.

Fontenrose, Joseph. "Travels With Charles," in John Steinbeck. pp. 137-138.

"TV Series Based on Travels With Charley Set; Steinbeck to Be Consultant," New York Times, April 22, 1963. p. 55.

The Vigilante
French, Warren G. "The Vigilante," in John Steinbeck. p. 83.

The Wayward Bus (1947)
Adams, J. Donald. New York Times Book Review, March 2, 1947. VII, p. 2.

Baker, Carlos. New York Times Book Review, February 16, 1947. VII, p. 1.

Clark, Eleanor. Nation, CLXIV (March 29, 1947),

370-373.

Cousins, Norman. Saturday Review of Literature, XXX (March 8, 1947), 22-23.

De Voto Bernard. New York Herald Tribune Books, February 16, 1947. p. 1.

Jackson, Joseph Henry. San Francisco Chronicle "This World," February 16, 1947. p. 17.

Kelley, H. Gilbert. Library Journal, LXXII (February 15, 1947), 321.

Lalley, J. M. New Yorker, XXIII (February 22, 1947), 87-90.

O'Malley, Frank. Commonweal, XLVI (April 25, 1947), 43-44.

Prescott, Orville. New York Times, February 17, 1947. p. 17.

_____. Yale Review, XXXVI (Summer, 1947), 765-766.

Smith, Harrison. Saturday Review of Literature, XXX (February 15, 1947), 14.

Watts, Richard Jr. New Republic, CXVI (March 10, 1947), 37-38.

Weeks, Edward. Atlantic, CLXXIX (March, 1947), 126-128.

Booklist, XLIII (February 15, 1947, 186.

Canadian Forum, XXVII (May, 1947), 45.

Manchester Guardian, November 29, 1947. p. 3.

New York Times, March 4, 1947. p. 23.

Time, XLIX (February 24, 1947), 118.

Times (London) Literary Supplement, November 29, 1947. p. 613.

Brown, John Mason. "Upright Bus," Saturday Review of Literature, XXX (April, 1947), 24-27.

"Film Studios Bid for New Novel, Wayward Bus," New York Times, November 3, 1946. II, p. 4.

Fontenrose, Joseph. "The Wayward Bus," in John Steinbeck. pp. 108-111.

French, Warren G. "The Wayward Bus," in John Steinbeck. pp. 143-148, Passim. Film, p. 30.

Gardiner, Harold C. "The Wayward Bus," in In All Conscience. New York: Hanover House, 1959. pp. 131-136.

Lisca, Peter. "The Wayward Bus," in The Wide World of John Steinbeck. pp. 231-247.

_____. "The Wayward Bus...A Modern Pilgrimage," SHC, pp. 281-290.
First appeared in his Ph.D. dissertation, "The Art of John Steinbeck," 1955.
See II, B, 1.

Richetts, Toni Jackson (Antonia Seixas). "John Steinbeck and the Non-Teleological Bus," What's Doing On the Monterey Penninsula, I (March, 1947).
Also in SHC. pp. 275-280.

Seixas, Antonia. See Richetts, Toni Jackson.

"Steinbeck's The Wayward Bus Was Listed As an Obscene Book By the House Select Committee on Current Pornographic Materials in Washington," Facts On File, XII (December 5-11, 1952), 397.
See II, A.

Walcutt, Charles C. "The Wayward Bus," in American Literary Naturalism, A Divided Stream. pp. 266-267.

Watt, F. W. "The Wayward Bus," in John Steinbeck. pp. 87-91.

"The Wayward Bus," Facts On File, XVII (June 27-

July 3, 1963), 216.
See II, A.

The White Quail
Fontenrose, Joseph. "The White Quail, " in John
Steinbeck. pp. 61-63.

French, Warren G. "The White Quail, " in John
Steinbeck. pp. 84-85, 120.

The Winter of our Discontent (1961)
Baker, Carlos. New York Times Book Review,
June 25, 1961. VII, p. 3.

Brynes, Asher. New Republic, CXLV (August 21,
1961), 24.

Butcher, Fanny. Chicago Sunday Tribune Magazine
of Books, June, 1961. p. 1.

Conterno, Larry. Catholic World, CXCIV (November,
1961), 125-126.

. DeMott, Benjamin. Hudson Review, XIV (Winter,
1961-62), 622.

, Didion, J.   National Review, XII (January 16, 1962),
33

Dvorak, Jermila. Books Abroad, XXXVI (Winter,
1962), 80.

Feeney, William J. Extension, LV (September, 1961),
15.

Gardiner, Harold C. America, LV (July 22, 1961),
554.

Harcourt, Peter. Time and Tide, LIX (June 22,
1961), 1031.

Hartt, J. N. Yale Review, LII (Winter, 1962), 305-
306.

Hicks, Granville. Saturday Review, XLIV (June 24,
1961), 11.

Hodgart, Matthew. New Stateman, LXI (June 30, 1961), 1052-1054.

Hutchens, John K. New York Herald Tribune, June 23, 1961. p. 21.

Jackson, Robert B. Library Journal, LXXXVI (June 15, 1961), 2339.

Keown, Eric. Punch, XX (July 5, 1961), 31.

Peterson, Virginia. New York Herald Tribune, June 25, 1961. p. 29.

Poling, Daniel A. Christian Herald, LXXXIII (November, 1961), 100.

Prescott, Orville. New York Times, June 23, 1961. p. 27.

Raven, Simon. Spectator, CCVI (June 30, 1961), 960.

Singer, Burns. Listener, LXV (June 29, 1961), 1145.

Weeks, Edward. Atlantic, CCVIII (July, 1961), 122.

Booklist, LVII (June 1, 1961), 606, 636.

Bookmark, XX (July, 1961), 234.

Christian Century, LXXIX (May 30, 1962), 693.

Christian Science Monitor, June 29, 1961, p. 7.

New Yorker, XXXVII (September 16, 1961), 177.

Newsweek, LVII (June 26, 1961), 96.

Time, LXXVII (June 23, 1961), 70.

Times (London) Literary Supplement, July 7, 1961. p. 413.

The Times (London) Weekly Review, July 6, 1961. p. 10.

Virginia Quarterly Review, XXXVII (Autumn, 1961),

Brynes, Asher. "A Man Who Lived with Failure,"
New Republic, CXLV (August 21, 1961), 24.
See also The Grapes of Wrath.

Cooperman, Stanley. "The Winter of our Discontent,"
in Review Notes and Study Guide to Steinbeck.
pp. 96-110.

Fontenrose, Joseph. "The Winter of our Discontent,"
in John Steinbeck. pp. 132-137.

French, Warren G. "Steinbeck's Winter Tale,"
Modern Fiction Studies, XI (Spring, 1965), 66-74.

Gerstenberger, Donna. "Steinbeck's American Waste
Land." Modern Fiction Studies, XI (Spring, 1965),
59-65.

Watt, F. W. "The Winter of our Discontent," in
John Steinbeck. pp. 102-103.

Others: Arranged By Miscellaneous Work
French, Warren G. "About Ed Ricketts (essay),"
in John Steinbeck. pp. 81, 136, 161, 172.

_____. "Critics, Critics, Burning Bright,"
(Essay in 1950), in John Steinbeck. p. 148.

_____. "How To Tell Good Guys from Bad
Buys" (Essay, 1955), in John Steinbeck. p. 28.

_____. "Lifeboat (film)," in John Steinbeck.
pp. 27, 163.

"Wrote Story of Lifeboat," Time, XLIII (January 31,
1944), 94.
See II, A.

French, Warren G. "Making of a New Yorker," in
John Steinbeck. pp. 19, 21, 167.

Butler, Frank. "A Medal for Benny, A Screen Play
Adapted from the Story of John Steinbeck and Jack
Wagner; Review," New Statesman, XXIX (May 26,
1945), 336.

Also in Newsweek, XXV (April 30, 1945), 96.
Also in Spectator, CLXXIV (May 25, 1945), 474;
Time, XXV (May 28, 1945), 54; Theatre Arts,
XXIX (June, 1945), 368.

French, Warren G. "Pipe Dream (musical comedy,
1955), " in John Steinbeck, pp. 30, 159-160.

"Pipe Dream, a Musical Comedy By Oscar Hammerstein II (Book and Lyrics) and Richard Rodgers
(Music) Based on Steinbeck's Novel, Sweet Thursday Was Produced, " Facts on File, XV (December
1-7, 1955), 403.

"Pipe Dream, " New York Times, November 27,
1955. II, p. 1; December 11, 1955. II, p. 1.

French, Warren G. "Secret Weapon We Were Afraid
to Use, " (Memoir, 1953), in John Steinbeck. p.
172.

_____. "Viva Zapata!" (film, 1950), in John
Steinbeck. p. 29.

"Viva Zapata!, A Story of the Mexican Indian Leader
Emiliano Zapata, a Screen Play By Steinbeck, "
Facts On File, XII (February 22-28, 1952), 67.

C. Reviews of Critical Books on John Steinbeck

Fontenrose, Joseph Eddy. John Steinbeck, An Intro-
duction and Interpretation. New York: Barnes and
Noble, 1963.
Reviews By
French, Warren G. American Literature, XXXVI
(May, 1964), 244.

Lisca, Peter. Western Humanities Review, XVIII
(Autumn, 1964), 384-385.

Virginia Quarterly Review, XL (Spring, 1964), lxi.

French, Warren G. (ed.). A Companion to The Grapes
of Wrath. New York: Viking Press, 1963.
Reviews By
G., C. American Literature, XXXVI (March, 1964),
121.

Jones, E. H. Library Journal, LXXXVIII (August, 1963), 2908; (November 15, 1963), 4492.

French, Warren G. John Steinbeck. New York: Twayne Publishers, 1961.
Reviews By
Booklist, LVIII (September 1, 1961), 14.

Hicks, Granville. Saturday Review, XLIV (August 12, 1961), 13.

Walbridge, E. F. Library Journal, LXXXVI (September 1, 1961), 2800.

Lisca, Peter. The Wide World of John Steinbeck. New Brunswick, N. J.: Rutgers University Press, 1958.
Reviews By
Gannett, Lewis. New York Herald Tribune Books, June 22, 1958. p. 4.

Hicks, Granville. Saturday Review, XLI (June 21, 1958), 49.

Kazin, Alfred. New York Times, May 4, 1958. p. 1.

Moore, Harry Thornton. American Literature, XXX (March, 1959), 388-389.

Moore, Harry Thornton. The Novels of John Steinbeck; A First Critical Study. Chicago: Normandie House, 1939.
Reviews By
Booklist, XXXV (May 15, 1939), 303.

J., H. J. Saturday Review of Literature, XX (June 10, 1939), 19.

New Yorker, XV (April 22, 1939), 78.

Tinker, E. L. New York Times, July 23, 1939. p. 15.

Tedlock, Ernest Warnock, and Wicker, Cecil Vivian (eds.). Steinbeck and His Critics; A Record of Twenty-Five Years. Albuquerque: University of

New Mexico Press, 1957.
Reviews By
Chicago Sunday Tribune, June 9, 1957. p. 4.

Moore, Harry T. New Republic, **CXXXVI** (May 27, 1957), 23.

Ray, David. Nation, **CLXXXIV** (April 20, 1957), 346.

Smith, E. T. Library Journal, **LXXXII** (April 1, 1957), 983.

Part III Bibliography

Beebe, Maurice, and Bryer, Jackson R. "Criticism of
John Steinbeck: A Selected Checklist," Modern Fiction
Studies, XI (Spring, 1965), 90-103.

Blanck, Jacob (ed.). "American First Editions," Publishers'
Weekly, CXXXI (April 17, 1937), 1701. ("Checklist of
John Steinbeck's Works" By Lawrence C. Powell.)

Burnett, Whit (ed.). "Steinbeck Bibliography," in The
World's Best: 105 Greatest Living Authors, New York:
Dial Press, 1950. p. 1155.

Cooperman, Stanley. Review Notes and Study Guide to
Steinbeck. New York: Monarch Press, 1964. "Bibliography," p. 112.

Dickinson, A.T., Jr. American Historical Fiction. New
York: Scarecrow Press, 1958. "Steinbeck," pp. 11,
20-21, 84, 147, 210, 232, 234. (1963 ed., pp. 96,
204.)

Ethridge, James M. (ed.). Contemporary Authors: A
Bio-Bibliographical Guide to Current Authors and Their
Works. Detroit: Gale Research Co., 1963. "Steinbeck,"
II, p. 184.

Fontenrose, Joseph. John Steinbeck: An Introduction and
Interpretation. (American Authors and Critics Series,
No. 8.)
New York: Barnes and Noble, 1963.
"Selected Bibliography," pp. 142-144.

French, Warren G. (ed.). A Companion to The Grapes of
Wrath. New York: Viking Press, 1960.
"Bibliography," pp. 229-235.

_____. John Steinbeck. New York: Twayne Pub-
lishers, Inc., 1961.
"Selected Bibliography," pp. 175-181.

Gannett, Lewis. John Steinbeck: Personal and Bibliographical Notes, A Pamphlet. New York: Viking Press, 1939.

Gerstenberger, Donna, and Hendrick, George. The American Novel 1789-1959: A Checklist of Twentieth Century Criticism. Denver: Allan Swallow, 1961. "John Steinbeck," pp. 225-230.

Hoffman, Hester R. (ed.). The Reader's Advisor and Bookman's Manual. 9th ed. New York: Bowker, 1960. "Steinbeck," pp. 993-994.

Humanities Research Center of the University of Texas. John Steinbeck: An Exhibition of American and Foreign Editions. Austin, Texas: The Center, 1963.

Jackson, Joseph Henry. "A List of Books By and Essays About John Steinbeck," in We Moderns, Catalogue Issued (No. 24). New York: Gotham Book Mart, 1920-1940. pp. 66-67.

Johnson, Merle. American First Editions. 4th rev. ed. Revised and edited by Jacob N. Blanck. New York: R. R. Bowker, 1942. Reprinted from Publishers' Weekly, CXXXI (April 17, 1937), 1701. (Checklist by Lawrence Clark Powell.)

Leary, Lewis Gaston. Articles on American Literature 1900-1950. Durham, N.C.: Duke University Press, 1954. pp. 278-279.

Lisca, Peter. "The Art of John Steinbeck: An Analysis and Interpretation of Its Development." Unpublished Ph.D. dissertation, The University of Wisconsin, 1955. "Bibliography," pp. 385-410.

_____. The Wide World of John Steinbeck. New Brunswick: Rutgers University Press, 1958. "A Working Checklist of Steinbeck's Published Work," pp. 310-314.

Millett, Fred B. Contemporary American Authors. New York: Harcourt, Brace, 1940. pp. 596-597.

Moore, Harry Thornton. The Novels of John Steinbeck: A First Critical Study. Chicago: Normandie House, 1939. "Bibliographical Checklist of First Editions," pp. 97-101.

Powell, Lawrence Clark. See Blanck, Jacob (ed.).

_____. "Toward a Bibliography of John Steinbeck,"
Colophone, III (Autumn, 1938), 558-568.
See also Johnson, Merle.

Quinn, Arthur Hobson, et al (eds.). The Literature of the
American People. New York: Appleton-Century-Crofts,
1951. p. 1102.

Singleton, R. H. (ed.). Two and Twenty, A Collection of
Short Stories. New York: St. Martin's Press, 1962.
pp. 239: "The Great Mountains,"; pp. 236-238 contain
bio-bibliographical information.

Spiller, Robert E., et al (eds.). Literary History of the
United States: Bibliography. 4 vols. 3rd ed. New York:
Macmillan, 1963.
"John Steinbeck," III, pp. 730-731; IV, pp. 192-193.

Steele, Joan. "John Steinbeck: A Checklist of Biographical,
Critical, and Bibliographical Material," Bulletin of
Bibliography and Magazine Notes, XXIV (May-August,
1965), 149-152, 162-163.

Tedlock, E. W., Jr., and Wicker, C. V. (eds.). Steinbeck
and His Critics: A Record of Twenty-Five Years.
Albuquerque: University of New Mexico Press, 1957.
"A Checklist of Steinbeck's Books," p. 310.

Wagenknecht, Edward Charles. Cavalcade of the American
Novel. New York: Henry Holt, 1942. pp. 554-555.

Watt, Frank William. John Steinbeck. (Evergreen Pilot
E. P. 13). New York: Grove Press, 1962.
"Bibliography," pp. 115-117.

Appendix

A. A List of Newspapers and Periodicals Indexed

America (National Catholic Weekly Review). W.

American Literature. Bi-M (November - May).

American Mercury. M.

American Quarterly. Q. (5 times a year).

The American Scholar. Q.

The American West. Q.

America; The American Motors Magazine. Bi-M.

Anglica (Japan). Q.

Antioch Review. Q.

Aoyama Gakuin University Studies in British and American Literature (Japan). Q.

Appalachian State Teachers College Faculty Publications (Formerly ASTC Bulletin). A.

Argosy (New York). M.

Atlantic Monthly. M.

Australian Quarterly (Australia). Q.

Beacon Study in Language and Literature (Kemmei Junior College, Japan). Q.

Book-of-the-Month-Club News. M.

Book Week; For Libraries and Schools. W.

Booklist (And Subscription Book Bulletin). Semi-M. (Formerly ALA Booklist).

The Booklover's Answer. Bi-M.

Bookmark. M (October-July). (New York State Library).

Books Abroad; (An International Literary Quarterly). Q.

Boston Globe. D.

Brief (Phi Delta Phi). Q.

British and American Literature (Kansei Gakuin University, Japan). Q.

The California Teachers' Association Journal. M. (September-May).

Canadian Forum (Canada). M.

The Catholic World. M.

Chicago Daily Tribune. D.

Chicago Sun Book Week. W.

Chicago Sunday Tribune Magazine of Books. W.

Christian Century. W.

Christian Science Monitor. D.

Christian Herald. M.

College English. M (October-May).

Collier's. W.

The Colophon (A Quarterly for Bookman). Q.

Colorado Quarterly. Q.

Columbia Literary Columns. 3 times a year.

Commentary. M.

Commonweal. W. [Bi-W. (July-September)].

Comparative Literature. Q.

Coronet. M.

Cosmopolitan. M.

Cresset, A Review of Literature. M. (September-June).

Current History. M.

Delphian Quarterly. Q.

Editor and Publisher. W.

English Journal. M. (September-May).

English and American Literature Studies (Aoyama Gakuin University, Japan). Q.

English Language and Literature Studies (Kyushu University, Japan). Q.

English Record. M.

Esquire. M.

Essays and Studies in British and American Literature (Tokyo Women's Christian College, Japan). Q.

Exercise Exchange, A Quarterly for the Interchange of Classroom Ideas among Teachers of Composition and Literature. Q.

Explicator. 10 times a year.

Extension, The National Catholic Monthly. M.

Ford Times. M.

Fortnightly (Britain). M.

Forum (Formerly Forum and Century). M.

Harper's Magazine. M.

The Hokkaido University Essays in Foreign Languages
and Literature (Japan). Q.

Holiday. M.

Good Housekeeping. M.

Huntington Library Quarterly. Q.

Illustrated London News (Britain). W.

Journal of Aesthetics and Art Criticism. Q.

The Journal of American Medical Association. W.

Journal of English and Germanic Philology (JEGP). Q.

Kansai Gakuin Times (Japan). Q.

Kenyon Review. Q.

Kyushu American Literature. Q.

Kyushu Institute of Technology Report (Japan). Q.

Ladies' Home Journal. M. [Bi-M. (January-July)].

Library Journal. Semi-M. [M. (July-August)].

Life. W.

Life and Letters Today (Britain). M (May-August).

Listener (Britian). M.

Literary Criterion. Bi-M.

Literary Digest. W.

London Magazine (Britain). M.

Lumina (Okayama University, Japan). A.

McCalls. M.

McNeese Review. M.

Manchester Guardian (Britain). W.

Massachusetts Review. Q.

160

Mississippi Quarterly.   Q.

Modern Fiction Studies.   Q.

Modern Monthly.   M.

Modern Quarterly (Britain).   Q.

The Monterey Beacon.   W.

The Monthly Record.   M.

Nation.   W. [Bi-W. (July-August)].

National Education Association Journal (NEA Journal).
M. (September-May).

National Review. W.

Negro History Bulletin.   M.

New Masses.   W.

New Republic.   W.

New Statesman (& Nation); an Independent Political
and Literary Review (Britain).   W.

New York Evening Post (Later New York Post).   D.

New York Herald Tribune Books.   W.

New York Times (Book Review).   W.

New York Times Magazine.   W.

New Yorker.   W.

Newsweek.   W.

North American Review.   Q.

Occident.   Q.

Pacific Historical Review.   Q.

Pacific Spectator; A Journal of Interpretation.   Q.

Perspectives (U. S.): A Quarterly of Literature and
the Arts.   Q.

Photography.   M.

Prairie Schooner.   Q.

PMLS; Publications of the Modern Language Association
of America.   5 times a year.

Princeton University Library Chronicle.   Q.

The Psychoanalytic Study of The Child (Britain).   A.

Publishers' Weekly. W.

Punch (Britain). W.

Reader's Digest. M.

Reading and Collecting. M.

Renascene; A Critical Journal of Letters. Q.

Reporter. Semi-M.

Reports of Studies (Otani Women's Junior College, Japan). Q.

Revues Des Langues Vivantes (Belgium). Bi-M.

Rocky Mountain Review. Semi-A.

St. Louis Post Dispatch (Sunday Pictures). W.

San Francisco Chronicle. D.

San Francisco News. D.

San Francisco Sunday Chronicle ("This World" Magazine). W.

Saturday Review. W. (Formerly Saturday Review of Literature).

Scholastic. W. (September-May).

Science and Society. Q.

Science Digest. M.

The Sewanee Review. Q.

South Atlantic Quarterly. Q.

Southern Review. Q.

Southwest Review. Q.

Soviet Review. Q.

Spectator (Britain). W.

Stage (Britain). W.

Stanford Lit. Q.

The Stanford Spectator. M.

Stetson Studies in the Humanities. A.

Survey Graphic. M.

Taira Technical Junior College Reports of Studies (Japan). Q.

Theatre Arts.   M.

Time.   W.

Time and Tide; Independent Weekly (Britain).   W.

Times (London) Literary Supplement (TLS) (Britain).   W.

The Times (London) Weekly Review (Britain).   W.

Today.   Bi-M.

Today's Health.   M.

Transatlantic Review, an International Literary Review.
Q.

Twentieth Century Literature: A Scholarly and Critical
Journal.   Q.

Unity, Fellowship and Character in Religion.   Bi-M.
(September-June).

The University of Kansas City Review (UKCR).   Q.

The University of Missouri Studies.   A.

Virginia Quarterly Review; A National Journal of
Literature and Discussion.   Q.

Vogue.   Semi-M. [M. (May-July, December)].

Way (U. S.).   M.

Western Folklore.   Q.

Western Review; A Literary Quarterly.   Q.

Wilson Library Bulletin (Formerly Wilson Bulletin for
Librarians).   M. (September-June).

Wings; The Literary Guild Review.   M.

Woman's Home Companion.   M.

Yale Review.   Q.

B. Key to Abbreviations

A.: Annual

D.: Daily

M.: Monthly

Q.: Quarterly

W.: Weekly

ALS: Autograph letter, signed

AMS: Autograph manuscript, signed

ANS: Autograph note, signed

APS: Autograph postcard, signed

d. w.: dust wrappers

LV: The Long Valley

Mi MS: Mimeographed manuscript

MS or MSS: Manuscript (s)

n. d.: no date

p.: page (s)

PM or "   ": Postmarked

PS: Postcard, signed

SHC: Steinbeck and His Critics, Ed. by Tedlock and Wicker (eds.).

TCS: Typed card, signed

TLS: Typed letter, signed

TPS: Typed postcard, signed

TMS or TMSS: Typed manuscript (s)

TSs: Typed script, signed

w. e.: with original envelope

164